I Send My Blankets Over You
Lessons of Love

*Poems, Stories and Songs for Healing,
Transformation and Co-Creating New Realities*

Volume One of
The Reflect upon the Rock Collection

Darya Funches, Ed.D.

1663 Liberty Drive, Suite 200
Bloomington, Indiana 47403
(800) 839-8640
www.AuthorHouse.com

© 2005 Darya Funches. All Rights Reserved.

Cover Design by Benny Assefa and Darya Funches

Text Illustrations by Malachi Daniels

Cover Quilt Made by Darya

REAP Unlimited Publishing, a Division of REAP Unlimited Corporation, has the exclusive rights to reproduce this work, electronically and otherwise.

Darya Funches has the copyright to each one of the poems, stories, songs and illustrations in this text, ©Darya Funches.

All rights reserved. None of this text, in whole or in part can be reproduced without written permission from REAP Unlimited. 1.866.785.REAP. www.reapunlimited.com and www.isendmyblanketsoveryou.com.
179 Thomas Road. Mossyrock, WA 98564

First published by AuthorHouse 12/05/05

ISBN: 1-4259-0333-9 (sc)

Library of Congress Control Number: 2005910333

Printed in the United States of America
Bloomington, Indiana

This book is printed on acid-free paper.

Dedicated to my daughter, Johari,
who is indeed a precious stone,
to my sister, Muriel, for her love and support,
and to those whom I have loved,
who have loved and not loved me.

Through my journeys with you, I have experienced the power of love.

For Unloved and Unloving Lovers

We don't always love those we think we should.
Love flows from within and through us—
The powers of a waterfall, the gentleness of crimson and gold leaves,
falling in sacred autumn woods.

No matter the person or outcome
of love ventured, lost or gained,
each attempt takes us closer Home,
where from Love each of us came.

In Divine Love, we die to be born again.
If we dare venture to love our God,
we become empty vessels, glowing yet plain.
Pure Love flows through our hollowed remains.

I Send My Blankets Over You – Lessons of Love

Foreword by Flo Aeveia Magdalena	xi
Acknowledgements	xv
AUTHOR'S PREFACE	xvii

Chapter One.
For Unloved and Unloving Lovers & Friends: 1973-2005

You're Just a Woman Creating Her Own Great Drama	3
Pure Love	5
The Power of Weakness	6
Next Time You Want a Woman Just for a Friend	8
Learn to Love the Shadow	10
There's No Such Thing as Casual Sex	12
I Made the Choice	14
Is She Your Friend?	15
They Find the Sweetest One	17
Players and the Played	18
Don't Lie to Me	20
Prisoner of the Past	21
The System May or May Not Love You Back	23
The Two of Rejection	26
There is Love for the Unloved Lover	28

Chapter Two.
Tests & Testimonies of Love: 1988-2005

Mother Root, Father Sky	33
Did I Ever Say?	34
I Prayed for You to Come	37
Measuring the Love	39
Everlasting, Ever Present Love	41
I Love You, I Worship God	42
Looking for that Mother-Father Kind o' Love	44
The Awakening	45
I Dreamed You Up	46

I Touched Love	48
What Made Me Love You?	49
Who, but You?	51
Come to Me at the First Snow	52
Feathers Fly Away	53
When My People Love You	54
I Love This Land and This Land Loves Me	55

Chapter Three.
At Last, Heal the Past: 1949-2005

Four Love Quests	61
No One Remembers, No One Tells	62
The Wound that Wants to be Healed	64
Child of Love's Hope	66
I Want to be a Better "Man" than My Daddy Was	69
You' de' Medicine Man	71
The Heart of a Babe Hidden	73
Love the Heart of a Tyrant	75
Love Thine Inner Me	76
Paint Me the Color of Love	78
Faith in Love	79
A Love Equation	80
I am the Prize	83
Be Love, Beloved	85

Chapter Four.
Love and Discernment: 1970-2005

Desire's Illusions, Love's Reality	89
Can You See Me?	90
If All Remains the Same	92
Dance of Commitment and Change	93
Circle the Triangle	94
Mr. Man	96
I Knew the Ice Would Come to Me	98
I've Been to the Movie, I've Seen the Picture Show	100

That's Not Spirit Telling You to Forget About Love	101
A Long Walk in the Desert	102
What's More Important, Control or Love?	104
A Gift is a Gift	106
What We're Offering, What We Want	107
Love's Trust	109

Chapter Five.
When it's Time to Go: 1977-2005

We Were	115
Psychic Wail	116
If It Hasn't Happened	118
Takin' Myself Out' the Game	120
How We Open and Close	121
Dear God, Can I Die Now?	124
I Wish You Well	126
Maybe it's Time to Let Go	127
Eight Poems for Endings	129

Chapter Six.
Calling Love Warriors: 1997-2005

Love is a Sacred Space	133
Rest the Weary Warrior and Warrioress	134
Twins Over Time	135
Sacred Woman, Sacred Man, Sacred Love	136
"He's" a Love Warrior	137
"She's" a Love Warrior	138
Bridging Waves and Worlds	139
Love is the Power	140
Fight, Flight and Light	141
The Ripple Effect	142
We're All Wading in the Water—A Living Poem	146
I Send My Blankets Over You	148

Chapter Seven.
Epilogue

Some of the Lessons of Love	157
The Reflect Upon The Rock Collection	159
About the Author	161
Other Works and Publications	163

FOREWORD
with Excerpts from
<u>I Send My Blankets Over You—Lessons of Love</u>

Love is the rock upon which we build our lives, relationships, families, communities, our world, and our interrelationship with all life. Love is the rock from which we base our hopes, dreams, and aspirations. It is the unmovable ground upon which we feel safe, joined, seen, known, desired, needed and held.

From our first breath we navigate our world moving instinctually toward that which will bring the most comfort, warmth, and stability—that which engenders tenderness, grace, and acceptance. Love. We believe that love comes from outside us and we have to find it, deserve it, keep it, and control it. Grappling, we move toward it, wanting unconditional union, and most times, find love laced with conditions, misunderstanding, disappointment, displeasure, betrayal, and emotional bankruptcy.

There is a space of emptiness that the perceived loss of love brings. We struggle! "Oh, it can't be true. He/she does love me! I know it, if only……" The page turns and there is emptiness, what now? "Who can I find to love me?" "How can I make this work?" "How can I make sure that I am not alone?" Our lives flatten as we acknowledge that we have to love first. We have to love ourselves, learn what love is and how it works. There is order to this—first I love myself, and then I can love another. First I forgive myself, and then I can forgive another. The poems Dr. Darya writes share specific experiences of recognizing this order.

From the inner depths of her own awareness, she offers us glimpses of the silver lining of the clouds of despair, loss, challenge, judgment, manipulation, blackmail, and seduction that love so often brings.

> "Don't lie to me, lie to someone who can't see.
> Lie to strangers or when there's no intimacy.
> When I discover lies from those I trust most,
> they become enemies I mistakenly brought close."

As we listen to the precise and pointed clarity of Dr. D's extraordinary eye, seeing within how we construct our world, we move to a more heightened self-awareness, self-acceptance, and fuller consciousness of patterns that continue in each love avenue we go down. There is projection, rejection, blind faith, delusion, pretense, obligation, Mother-need, Father-need, and sexual entanglement.

> "Heal the self, if new results you seek to find,
> 'cause in love we're all being paid in kind."

She brilliantly reflects the ways we seduce ourselves into believing that what we need sits right in front of us—if only we can be smaller, bigger, more patient, more available, tolerate more, need less, do more.

> "Love may not appear to match images in the brain.
> You must discern entry into love's diverse terrain.."

Her poems bring to life how the wounds of our small hearts stay with us as we grow bigger and bigger bodies. She uncovers those initial hurts and lays them out, her poignant images penetrating the layers of our childhood, adolescence, and adult years, bringing us to acknowledge, "Yes! Yes! That's right! How did she know? Me, too. WOW."

> "Fear blocks the inner eye's sun,
> triggering images past for the moment begun."

> "For there are no dark places that go forever unseen,
> since we live on a universal projection screen."

Painlessly she rips apart our defenses leaving us grateful, restored, understood, and stronger. Just seeing the truth absolves the lie. Just being in the presence of the wisdom she unfolds offers us the knowledge that the wisdom is in us, too.

We see the Love path drawn out through her words and the true identity of the mother, father, sister, brother, lover, and child self. We see the twisted and the straight, the tortured and the cured, the possible and the actual. We see it all.

> "Relationships are perfect mirrors, you know.
> He/she has held the energy for you to unfold
> the whole of who you are, ever evolving star.
> Homeward come all your exiled parts,
> no matter the outcomes, no matter the starts."

Going further, she shows how we co-create these learnings with those we used to blame, and ritualize our pain, again and again. She calls us to acknowledge from the deepest space within, that we are only slaves to love who spin and spin and spin.

As we see, we choose to close the gap inside, to bring the learning nearer, to open the heart to the potential, and to guide the soul ever more clearly home to rest within us, within the heart that we strengthen through our own becoming.

> "Be Love and you are Beloved.
> You are the Fruit and you are the Seed.
> Be Love, Beloved.
> Let this be your Creed."

Then, introducing spirit, soul, interconnectedness, and grace, Dr. D tells us about the greatest love, the broadest gateway to peace, understanding, and self-honoring. Bringing forth the wisdom she has gathered in as a practitioner in personal, corporate, and spiritual work, she unifies themes of self, family, community, life streams, business, the world, and the universe. She relates these Love themes to a new order, and a much promised and prophesized place awaiting our choice and memory, individually and collectively. This place is the promise of oneness that becomes available when we no longer seek to love from ego, control from mind, or attach to outcome—available when we seek to love not only as a psyche, but also as a soul.

Dr. D's intention and accomplishment is showing us how this is done. She lays out for us a road to freedom and vision. She leads us to own our creative energy and teaches us how to share and collaborate, transforming the habitual and conditioned:

> "It is best not to discern realities with emotions
> or even with desires, for these waters and fires
> are fed by the psyche, and not Divinely inspired."

> "That's why I send my blankets over you,
> so your heart will never again be broken,
> once you have the courage to let it open."

<u>I Send My Blankets Over You—Lessons of Love</u> is a gift of Love. Purely and clearly, it calls us to see, allows us to acknowledge, encourages our release, shows us how to move on, invites us to come together and join hands with all those who walk with us, and gives us acceptance of others and ourselves. We see Love in all its many facets and all its many expressions, freely, with no residue, need or fear. We see the potential of all humans to grow as one organism under the Great Spirit of the Heart, and we respond. We respond organically, and we grow, expand, understand, and celebrate.

We celebrate our heart, our vision, and our humanity, and then reflect on that humanity. Perhaps for the first time, we see opportunities to transform our families and social systems through the heart, accessing the ground of our Love as the rock upon which to build these new models of being.

Dr. D remarkably offers us a new vision of the human drama, transforming us into sacred warriors of peace and light. It happens as we read, recite, and reflect. It's naturally occurring. We sigh. We acknowledge. We let down, we let go of the way it was. Memories of oneness and potential surface from within the deep recesses of our psyche, and the revelations startle us into accordance, and we flow in the grace and possibility of Love's blanket.

    Flo Aeveia Magdalena
    Author of <u>I Remember Union</u> and <u>Sunlight on Water</u>

Acknowledgements

I share this work with gratitude for support of those from the heavens and earth who encourage, strengthen, and assist me. The prayers, physical assistance and moral support of those who have listened, provided funds, and who believed that sharing this work was worthwhile to them and others has been essential. Thanks to my immediate family for their faith in me, particularly my sister, Muriel, and three of my daughters, Johari, Alona, and Tizita, who have stayed especially close to me as I have gone under the Rock to write. I have certainly learned about the challenges and joys of Love with family from my parents, Joseph and Myrtle Funches, my brothers, Jeaux and Vaughn, and my nieces, nephews and cousins.

I am equally grateful to extended family and friends—coming from all directions. Special thanks to those who stayed close to me while I rested, struggled and toiled upon the Rock and while the Rock rested, struggled and toiled upon me. Brenda Mc., Sylvan H., C. Boyer, Flo Aeveia, Jayn S., Mac Ruka, Buck and Vicki G.H., J. Carter, Kobie and Tizita, Jean K. L., David and Willetta, Dave F., Tucker, Bob M., Eunice P.C., Roberta B., Beverly and Elton W., Niyonu, Sandy T., Betsy and Buff, John and Vickie, Bebop, Carolyn H., Rod and Linda, Nan C., Tyler W., Susan T., Sister Ruth, Gar and Marian, Pat S.M., Joyce O., Rita and John, Lisa M., Bruce C., Marc B., Peji, Sarah B., Kathleen J., Laura V.L.H., Sam Y., Adrienne and Michael, Edgar J., Freda and Sue, Vincent C., Mary Lou M., Carl M., Patricia P., Rosalind and Russell, Jill and Walter, Alison and Jean-Marie, Cora and Ken, Lennox J., Belinda and David, Regina and Q., Julie R.-S., Jessie C., Heidi and Jalene, Dodie and Jim, Cassandra and Trent, and finally Good Horse Nation—you've all provided a lifeline or touchstone at some point for me in the past seven years. I am grateful to you and to those I do not have space to mention.

I appreciate the insights and continuity of Jayn A. Stewart in editing some of my work over the years, the artistry of Malachi Daniels in the illustrations, and Benny Assefa's design skills and Sylvan Henoch's artistic consultations on the cover. Participants in the "Reflect upon the Rock Gatherings" at Mossyrock Landing have encouraged me to bring the work forward for Volume One and the larger collection. Special thanks to those who took the time to review earlier drafts of the entire text of Volume One: Dr. Jean Kantambu Latting, Flo Magdalena, Dr. Maxine Mimms, Sylvan Henoch, Minister Isa Nichols, Dr. David Thomas, Rebecca Wright, Mario Giovanni, Muriel Funches, Johari Funches-Penny, and Good Horse Nation. My long-time friend and colleague, Jean Latting, reviewed and commented upon every poem or story. My daughter, Johari, proofed each one of the "final revisions."

Clients, teachers, counselors and students throughout my career have helped me, directly or indirectly, remember about Love, life, Spirit, creativity and transformation. You know who you are. I give thanks to Creator, Grandmothers and Grandfathers of all directions, Unity Center of Christianity, The Ones with No Names, Keepers of the Akashic Records, John Carter and the Gestalt Institute's OSD Community, the REAP Learning Community, Ramtha, Mary Thunder, Mac Wiremu Ruka, Grand Shaykh Nazim, Buck Ghost Horse, and Cannup Yuha.

AUTHOR'S PREFACE

How this Book Came to Be

I set out to write several books about the models and techniques I had developed during my career for change agents, leaders, and others interested in transformation and change. The result was several books, including a collection of poems and stories, the first of which is this book, <u>I Send My Blankets Over You,</u> a book about Love. It was not quite what I had in mind. Yet it is as much a pure expression of me and my work as a structured organizational intervention would be. It is a result of my healing journeys with Love. I wrote it to awaken us to the need for Pure Love at all levels of existence. I wrote it to support the healing journeys of others. Here is how the book came to be.

Like many people, since I was a small child, I wrote stories, plays and poems as a way to express dreams, visions and emotional experiences. Later this type of writing was a hobby and a tool to supplement my primary work with clients. In 1997, after 26 years of an intense career, I needed a sabbatical. I decided to take a year off for rest, reflection and writing. My Mother had passed in the change from 1993 to 1994 and I needed time to grieve her transition, which came suddenly. Once I started the sabbatical in 1997, my Father became ill and passed in 1998. I met and fell in love with a man in 1997, a month after my former fiancé passed and soon before my Father crossed a few months later. Shortly after meeting this new man, I lost one of my best friends. I began to write more seriously, and to write whatever came first. A few years later, my brother died in 2003. And I was still on sabbatical.

Experiences with loss and my new love interest triggered wounds that needed to heal, despite the significant healing work I did earlier in life. <u>I Send My Blankets Over You</u> [ISMBOY] began with this process. It was my first experience with unrequited romantic love. With deep work, my experience transformed beautifully into Self Love and Pure Love. My insights during this time catalyzed connections to the Love we need to cultivate at all levels—individual, couples, groups, communities, organizations and nations. Much of the human drama of separation can be described as "being unloved" and/or "being unloving." We have our own wounds, joys, and lessons of love to learn at all levels of systems.

The sabbatical was a journey inward. With each spiral inward, I went more deeply and reached more expansively. Having asked for guidance for what was next in my work, I heard the call to take my work to the people, making it more available to everyone. As I asked for direction on this massive task, and as I laid down the mantle of professional work, all else fell away. The catalytic experience of love, and all the other transitions in my life, including becoming an elder in my family, took me to the poems and stories in ISMBOY. Amazingly, the intended one year sabbatical became a seven year sabbatical, now ending with this book.

Transformations Before the Sabbatical

As part of becoming a mother in 1970, I had one of my greatest personal transformations. I found myself progressively aspiring to love myself and others unconditionally. As part of my childhood spiritual experiences, this aspiration was with me even in the 50's. In the 70's it became more pressing, however. The more I aspired in this direction, the more I needed to resolve my wounds of love and acceptance.

In the 80's, I began developing my own approach to transformation and change, influenced by the need to work deeper and faster for positive results with large systems and large numbers of individuals. I developed the "Three Gifts of the Organization Development Practitioner" model, focused on "Discernment, Heart and Presence" for effective use of self as a change agent and leader. At that time, I also developed the "REAP Unlimited Model for Creating New Realities." I was a successful practitioner and a leader in the field, who spent my time working with clients, creating concepts, and writing. I spent minimal time turning my work into publications for the public, however. So my work was only available to clients and some colleagues.

This work was a transformation, bringing me to work more from the inside out, and bringing my parallel existences into crossing one another: spirit and business, politics and technology, science and art. The more I transformed myself, the more my work with clients deepened and expanded, and the more my leadership in the field expanded.

In the 70's and 80's I found myself co-creating tests of not being loved and tests of being loving—so that any residual aspects of not loving myself could arise and be resolved. Through these tests, I began to see connections between early gifts and wounds, the programs and patterns we develop, and the fabric of experiences we develop in community, friendships, love, family, nations, leadership and business. ISMBOY, and the <u>Reflect upon the Rock Collection</u> on the whole, are ways of sharing slices of what I have learned about these connections, using myself and others in my life as examples.

I have always perceived the work I do as a means to help and serve others, and also as a means to develop, grow and change myself. Working to help organizations and others grow and transform without doing so myself is asking others to do what I am not willing to do. I prefer to ask people to go some place that I am also willing to go.

Consulting to and leading change in organizations with integrity requires people to stand in and speak their truths as part of expressing their own needs and the highest good of the whole. I've often thought of myself as in "The Truth Business," which can be useful in the context of organizational politics. The more a person is driven by his or her psychological wounds, the more challenging it is to speak one's truth and experience the Whole.

I drew clients to me who would trigger the Lessons of Love I needed to learn. Likewise, I drew lovers, mates, family and colleagues who triggered the lessons I needed. We all magnetize the experiences we need to resolve our pasts and evolve our futures.

Some of these experiences are the subject of the 88 poems and stories in this book.

You May Ask: "What's Love Got to Do With It?"

I say, "Everything." We begin and end with Love. First we learn about love and acceptance from those in our immediate environment, influencing how we perceive ourselves and the sense we make about all that is around us. We interpret much of life at home and at work based on how we love ourselves and others. Second, our Ways of Love influence how and whether we trust self, others and Spirit to provide what we want and need. Third, we develop our awareness as co-creators in the lives we are living.

We realize that how we see the world, how we are in it, and what we do are key to making our reality every moment. We learn how to unfold what is right for this moment, for this time.

Love is fundamental. It is in the bedrock of our beliefs and assumptions. Our early experiences with love, or lack thereof, grow roots for our patterns of behavior. Yet, love defies definition except by its unique vibration. It is used to refer to everything from physical appetites to spiritual bliss. For some of us, this bedrock called love was a series of slippery stones in a river bed of swampy water. For some, the love foundation was jagged rocks beneath rapid waters. For some it was a cleansing pumice stone amidst a warm bath. Still for others, the bedrock of love is a calm, strong and powerful resting place to gain strength and comfort. All these experiences help us become who we are.

Many of the challenges we experience at home and at work, in our communities and families, in our business and religious worlds, in our country and international relations—have to do with the experience of and attachment to separation. We often miss the experience and appreciation of wholeness and love from moment to moment. Fragments of our lives yearn to integrate and begin to come together when we address how we love and how we don't. We heal old wounds, face deep truths, realize our souls' dreams and reveal more of who we truly are and are born to be. Then we have more positive impact as parents, leaders, followers, helpers, artists, teachers, learners, lovers and change agents. We begin and end with Love.

Why do We Do the Things We Do?

In <u>ISMBOY</u>, I want to help us look at our ways of seeing, knowing, being and doing Love. In the 1980's I introduced a concept called "Three Levels of Change," as a way of examining the depth of changes organizations, leaders and others were pursuing. It was a tool to examine "Ways of Seeing and Knowing, Ways of Being and Ways of Doing." The ways become clear as we translate these into specific patterns, including trigger events, assumptions and interpretations of events/experiences, emotions and specific behaviors and actions.

The patterns are programs, originated in historical experiences, our own and our ancestors'. Look at four examples of patterns below which express aspects of the program in the form of run-on sentences:

1. "When I love someone and he/she does not instantly return the feelings, I think or assume I am not attractive or good enough, but that if I work hard enough I can get what I want from him/her, and if I give the person everything he/she wants and needs, he/she will eventually love me in return. I feel anxious and fearful that I will be abandoned for another person if I don't get on the job to pursue the object of my affection, and I feel hurt when he/she doesn't choose me over others. I take the initiative and keep working hard to get the love I want from this person."

2. "When I have the opportunity to create a new product for a client, I think or assume that what I create won't be as good as what someone else can do, that what I create won't be worth the money I ask the client to pay for it, and that it will take me too long to produce something useful and valuable to the client. I feel afraid, nervous and inadequate to do the work and ashamed that I am not doing my share to provide for my family. I procrastinate in competing for projects and copy ideas from others who I assume are more creative than I am."

3. "When I enter a new organization that is predominantly Caucasian, I think or assume others will perceive me as "not good enough" or as incompetent at what I do because they are not accustomed to having African American women consultants work with them in the areas that I do. I begin to feel resentful, and angry and afraid of failing. I do the work, making sure I am super-competent and ready for a potential dangerous war-zone, and hold back really sharing myself fully because I am protecting myself."

4. "When someone I like is attracted to me and pursues me, I think or assume that I am in danger, that I am likely to be hurt, that it is good but dangerous to be appealing to a man I like, and I feel nervous and anxious, afraid and distrusting of the other person and myself. As a result, I withhold my feelings, dress to make myself look less attractive, avoid contact when being pursued, and eat more to reduce my anxiety in the short-term."

Each of the patterns above is rooted in some key incident[s] from earlier in life, and how the people in the examples responded to these. Patterns persist with some payoffs and prices to the individual and others. In these situations, people learned to diminish what they have to offer and to make others more valuable, powerful and worthy. The consequences are often the opposite of what the person really wants to happen.

The third example is a previous, not current, pattern of mine that I learned from traveling the highways of Mississippi as a small child with my family. We couldn't use the restrooms at the service stations along the way because of racist laws at the time in Mississippi and other states. I recall thinking that life was dangerous away from home and our people, as I watched my parents make efforts to keep us safe while traveling at night. I sensed their concern about the danger we were in, and we made this nocturnal journey frequently.

As I began to heal from wounds I experienced in early racist and sexist situaions, I began to love myself enough to be more free and authentic, whether I was in a new organization or not, and whether it was a predominantly Caucasian organization or not.

The power of an incident such as this is in the foundation of our Ways of Seeing and Knowing, beyond what is rational or explicit. Rationally, I had been raised to have confidence in myself and to know that prejudice and racism meant there was something wrong with the people and systems that behaved this way. Unconsciously, however, I responded to the behaviors and danger I sensed in the presence of my protectors, my parents.

During these times, if there was car trouble, my parents knew to get to a telephone booth and look up the closest A.M.E. Church [African Methodist Episcopal]. The Minister for such a church would be African American, someone we could rely on in the middle of the night for help, and not just because we were also A.M.E.

I internalized this sense of danger and carried it with me unconsciously once I began to enter predominantly Caucasian environments. I was stunned when I recognized the difference in my authenticity and quick effective use of self in systems that were filled primarily with People of Color. Understandably, this was like the familiarity of home. As I healed from this wound early in my career, it helped me work effectively in all systems and allowed me to assist others with similar patterns.

The fourth pattern example is also from my life, based on my experiences with molestation. This type of pattern is rooted in being violated by one's "protectors," leading to feeling unworthy, not good enough and unsafe, and leads to distrust of self and others in intimate relationships.

From our wounds, we appear to separate from ourselves, sometimes from God, and from others. Yet our wounds bring great lessons and opportunities to grow, evolve and assist others. Healing brings a reunion of the Self and with all that there is.

You may do your own healing as a part of reading this book. You may also pursue additional support in person with professionals.

Connections to Organizations

In my consulting practice over the years, three of the commonalities that stand out to me about how people perceive themselves and their workplaces are:

1. Most people want to be authentic at work. Yet they think they can't truly show who they are and be who they are in the context of their organizations. Their perception is that if they show who they are, the consequences will be negative. In some corporate organizations, this is so pervasive that it makes you wonder who is showing up for work. For the most part, it is not the authentic self of most of the people there on the job. This is a challenge for innovation, creativity and performing well in multi-cultural environments.

2. Most people think of themselves as honest but don't think honesty is a strong part of their organizations. Many think being honest in organizations is suicidal. There is often a covert agreement that one of my clients aptly described as, "I'll lie to you if you'll lie to me." Anyone who thinks he/she can be honest and succeed is considered naïve, reckless, stupid or as having substantial power based on position, relationships, ownership or role. In other words, "He or she can afford to speak the truth." "Truth speakers" are heroes and heroines in our society, as well as victims and martyrs.

3. Most people would rather work where they feel a match between themselves and the organization, yet many people would really rather be somewhere else other than where they are working. This often changes as soon as the system increases its integrity with the people and the people increase their integrity with the system.

As in relationships with individuals and families, we often measure the love in organizations by whether we are getting what we want and how we're doing compared to how others are doing. Often, we do not measure the love we experience within and express outwardly. Even those who are only at work to get the task done and get money to take care of loved ones express patterns at work triggered by love's wounds. We may appear to be free from attachment to having emotional needs met in the workplace. Detachment from what others think, want or need works for some people who have this approach. Appearances can also be deceiving.

Pure Love has more potential to heal what appears broken and to move us and the systems we co-create to be healthy, sustainable and regenerative. Our souls are already sparked with the Pure Love of Creation. And we are Whole where we appear to be broken.

Although many of us have mental and emotional separations between our domains of love and family from our world of business and work, the first world has a significant impact on the second one. Organizations are beginning to acknowledge the significant impact of the personal realm on the organization and are beginning to legitimize the resolution of personal issues and personal growth as a significant part of leadership and employee development, increasing morale, creativity, performance and productivity.

Why Is This Your Time to Read This Book?

You may already know the answer to this question. If not, the answer may appear soon, once you are in the reading process. When you are ready for a teacher, a teacher appears. When you are ready to heal, good vehicles for healing appear. When you are ready to lead yourself into the next wave of your life, the right book or other resource appears. It is now time to do the personal work that takes you to the next phase of your growth.

Know who you are, why you are here, and what you agreed to do. Recognize the "medicine" with which you were born, poured into you as you came through your birth. Love and accept the "medicine" because it is from your life experiences and how you are learning to understand and interpret these. These are unique gifts, present in your inner experience and outer expression in the world. This is who you are—beyond roles, goals, work, location and relationship.

Once you come to recognize your medicine and to love and accept your medicine, the time comes to take your own medicine. There are people and Spirits who can always assist in our healing but our healing comes from within. Deep in our bones, when we are ready to make a change, all of a sudden a door will appear. Learning to take our own medicine is part of what is required to work with others as a leader, teacher, counselor, healer and parent.

> "Power's the medicine we're all makin'
> from the medicines we're all takin'.
> We're all born with gifts to be wakin',
> to use, and not be forsakin'."
> From "You' de' Medicine Man," Chapter Three

> "What if Love is the Power, moving everything—
> the thunder of the heavens, the blooming in the Spring?
> What if Love is the Power, holding all life brings—
> the movement of the waters and the song the swan must sing?"
>
> From "Love is the Power," Chapter Six

Your Ways of Loving are "medicine" you've been making all your life.

The Focus is on Pure Love

I explore the nature and importance of Pure Love to our mundane and spiritual lives and to our quality of life on the whole. In part, I do this by contrasting and comparing Pure Love to the other dynamics we have come to call "love." We normally equate "love" with our romantic adventures, which are also wonderful. These adventures, and our experiences with others, give us windows, if we look, into areas needing healing, resolution and evolution. These windows help us fulfill our life purposes. Through examples of my own and others' personal journeys of being loved and unloved, and being loving and unloving, you may glimpse your own strengths, patterns, wounds, healing resolutions and potentials.

What is the Source of the Poems, Songs and Stories?

People often ask me, "Where do these poems come from?" The best answer I can give is, "from within." Some pieces come through prayer and meditation, whereas others reflect my experience or observations in the world. I listen to Spirit when I write, and I write about what I see, hear and feel.

Some poems, such as "You're Just a Woman Creating Her Own Great Drama," were inspired by my need to find a way to communicate something to women friends who seemed to be going through the same type of experience at the same time. After having repetitious conversations for months, feeling as if my perspectives on the subject were not getting through, I sat down and wrote this poem. "You're Just a Woman Creating Her Own Great Drama" turned out to be one of the most popular poems I've ever written. It helped some friends see the humor in what they were doing and expecting. Of course, I've had my own experiences with this subject too, giving me the insight to write the poem.

The poem is not a criticism of the man in question; it challenges the expectations and motives of the woman, a perspective many women find helpful, including me. There are similar poems I wrote based on laughing at my own behavior, such as "I Want to Be a Better Man than My Daddy Was," a deep, yet funny look at developing my inner male as a feminine woman.

Then there are the poems inspired by particular relationships that helped me learn my lessons of love, like "Who, But You?", "Everlasting, Ever Present Love", "I Love You, I Worship God," "We Were," "You' de' Medicine Man," "A Long Walk in the Desert," "Twins Over Time," "Child of Love's Hope" and the title poem, "I Send My Blankets Over You."

Some of the poems are composites, reflecting experiences of different people. Examples of this are "Can I Die Now," "The System May or May Not Love You Back," and "What We're Offering, What We Want." The System May or May Not Love You Back reflects the sentiments of many internal and external change agents when they don't feel appreciated or valued by the organizations that seek their assistance. It can be just as challenging for professionals at work as it is for people in their personal lives to be unloved by the objects of their affections.

There are also poems inspired by larger social and system issues. For example, "We're All Wading in the Water" is a living poem, inspired by the events and people most involved in Hurricane Katrina. "The Ripple Effect" is a poem I wrote in 1993 as a response to a request for my Vision of Diversity in the Future.

Many of the lessons of love addressed here apply not just to two people, but to groups of people in relationship to one another. Facing and resolving our Lessons of Love, and the polarities love can create, prepare us for being more empowered co-creators in our lives and in the world. Whether we want to master self-liberation, unity, manifestation, clear sight, leadership or transcendence—we have to address our Lessons of Love to be self-realized people. Many of the challenges within organizations and society are rooted in unresolved issues of genuine self-worth, self-love and lack of love and appreciation for humanity and all of life. There are six major chapters and the Epilogue, covering this range of love.

CHAPTER ONE. For Unloved and Unloving Lovers and Friends. Chapter One speaks to the part of us that has ever experienced being "unloved" or "unloving." I introduce the notion of Pure Love through the poem of that same title, and through the opening poem, "You're Just a Woman Creating Her Own Great Drama." The rest of Chapter One demonstrates some of the limiting patterns underlying our Ways of Love, which lead to some of the dramas we co-create in our relationships. The poems are not about victims or persecutors, but about what we co-create in our relationships. You may begin to reflect upon your strengths and patterns of intimacy, control and affection. You may see the assumptions and motives driving your behavior. Unloved and unloving lovers can examine their own shadows and levels of self-love.

Whether we feel we have missed love and acceptance from a sibling, a parent, or children, for example, the patterns we develop as parents, teachers, leaders, lovers and spouses may need our current attention.

In this Volume, I explore my own journey, my observations of others' journeys and their experiences as well. I am asking, "What is Pure Love's relationship to the evolution of human consciousness, our mundane existence, and our quality of life on the whole?" In part, I do this by contrasting and comparing Pure Love to the other dynamics we have come to call "love", the romantic entanglements that give us windows to attend Love's School. Then I expand Love to examples in broader life.

CHAPTER TWO. Tests and Testimonies of Love. Our greatest tests of love may follow our greatest prayers for love. Our greatest testimonies of love may follow our greatest tests. This Chapter focuses on our intentions, expressions, needs and desires in love. Tests surely arrive, challenging our readiness, willingness and worth to give and receive what we say we want in love. Our testimonies of love are windows into our preferred ways of loving and being loved. The tests we encounter are the ways our loved ones tell whether and how we are doing meeting their preferred ways of loving and being loved.

Once we think we have resolved a personal issue of love while being in a relationship with another, we are sure to meet a test that gives us the opportunity to demonstrate to ourselves and others what we have learned. These tests also serve to point the way to additional healing that we need to address deeper causes of our issues. We can see whether and how we got the lesson involved.

CHAPTER THREE. At Last, Heal the Past. This Chapter takes us further into the roots of what needs healing to evolve more on the journey to self-love and Pure Love. It includes poems illustrating how we use relationships to heal from the past, how past wounds influence our choices, and how we can heal. As you read this chapter, you may explore the roots and origins of your own Ways of Love and how these affect you at work, home and beyond.

One of the themes in the book is to recognize our quests for clarity about four aspects of our lives. The poem, "Four Quests of Love," introduces these four aspects: the wound, the lie, the dream and an exiled aspect of self. I share specific insights about my own love journeys, illustrating how I developed certain patterns based on specific wounds. I share my own journey into forgiveness and resolution, and poems that bring a balm for the wounds, such as "Paint Me the Color of Love." Some poems also bring tools for releasing the past. Self-Love is key to the healing process. I'll be the first to admit that I used to think of Self-Love the way I think of giving oneself a good massage: "If I've got to do it myself, what's the point?" My own healing journeys have led me to see things differently now.

CHAPTER FOUR. Love and Discernment. This Chapter brings forth challenges and opportunities for growth through loving others. In particular, I raise the significance of developing our discernment—our abilities to see ourselves and others clearly—in the context of love, despite all the conventional perspectives on the blindness of love. Pure Love is not blind, although there are certainly stages of falling in love that we can all attest to as contributing to poor sight. Our attempts to meet our needs and our attachment to certain outcomes, however, drive this poor sight. Through Pure Love, we actually come to see more clearly, rather than through eyes distorted by our emotional needs. There is an invitation here, and pathways, to travel to a place of awareness where we can love more fully and perceive more accurately.

CHAPTER FIVE. When it's Time to Go. This Chapter is more about recognizing one's own inner direction than it is about any set guidelines for the choice to go. With some humor and compassion, I address the grief, relief and growth in recognizing the time and acting upon it, whether or not we are initiating the ending. We all co-create the beginnings, middles and endings of our relationships. We only have to uncover and acknowledge how and why we contribute as we do.

CHAPTER SIX. Calling Love Warriors. This Chapter is an invitation to those who are dedicated pupils in Love's School. Here I endeavor to paint a picture of this calling and pictures of those who may have it, using the masculine and feminine principles rather than people as specific examples. Some of us feel we have enjoyed and been challenged in our Lessons of Love. Chapter Six encourages us to continue and call forth others who have the same dedication as we do to passing our love initiations. Certainly, Pure Love is not for the faint-hearted.

CHAPTER SEVEN. Epilogue. Finally, there is a poem which sums up the book in the final chapter.

SOME SUGGESTIONS FOR READING THIS BOOK: ACTIVE READING TIPS

You may wish to read at your leisure without any particular structure. The tips below are for those people who prefer some support. The Companion Book will have a variety of exercises and guidelines to assist readers who want to do personal transformation work with the poems and stories. Although many of the stories are about me and others, these raise shared human experiences, such as love, loyalty, loss, joy, betrayal, desire, abandonment, violence, bliss and ecstasy.

Keeping track of what comes up for you and what you want to do about it places you squarely in a conversation with yourself about your own Ways of Loving.

1. Keep a journal when you are reading I Send My Blankets Over You. In the journal, make notes of your thoughts, feelings, emotions, and relevant examples from your own life. Note the similarity and difference from how you tend to respond, compared to the characters in the poem or story.

2. Select a poem or story to focus on for the day, week or month. Read it every morning and every evening, making notes. Notice deeper and alternative meanings and how these relate to your life. How does the poem/story support you in your daily life? After the period of focus, write a response to the poem, based on your own experience and conclusions.

3. For a poem you need/want to learn more about, use an illustration from the book, or create one for yourself. Use the image to guide a meditation on the poem or story in the morning or evening.

4. Experiment with a recommendation included in a particular poem for a day, 3 days or a week. Some of the poems suggest taking on a particular way of looking at a situation or specific exercises to do [A Love Equation].

5. Enact all the parts of a poem or story by yourself or with others. This type of active experimentation can be enlightening. Feel free to express what the writer or the characters do not say explicitly in the poem, as well as expressing what the writer/characters say explicitly.

6. Make notes of what you appreciate about your Ways of Love and the ways you perceive having been loved. Be sure to express this appreciation to the people involved, even if they are not physically present. Use one of the poems here to express this appreciation, if it is appropriate, or write your own.

7. If and when you come across a wound within that is not yet healed, it is good to pursue professional and/or spiritual help in your healing process. You've opened the doorway for the healing to occur. It may be helpful to work with someone who does in-depth healing work, using approaches beyond "talk therapy." Additional resources are also helpful, such as books and CD's for healing traumatic experiences.

8. Use the "Four Love Quests" as a mantra in between reading selections in the book. As I neared completion of the book, I could hear these four quests over and over again. The four quests are part of our search for Love and its Unifying Power in the form of four questions. Coming up with your own answers is a significant part of the journey. What is the wound that never fully healed? What is the great lie and the truth the lie concealed? What is the urgent dream yearning to be made real? What is the part of you wanting most to be revealed?

9. For the sake of learning, adjust the poems and stories to fit your spiritual, religious, sexual and/or cultural orientations. To get the most from the poem or story, it may be helpful for you personally to adjust the language to fit your orientations and preferences. This includes changing pronouns from she to he or vice versa, changing God to Goddess, or Spirit to Holy Spirit, or Jesus to Grandfather or Universe to Lord. I am not saying that these terms are equivalent. I am only encouraging you to use language and images that fit who you are and what you believe.

10. Join a gathering online or in person about one or more poems, using the book website. Discussion with others can be a source of insight and support.

Many of the poems are designed to provide information, increase awareness or be therapeutic. Depending on where you are on your healing journey, healing may spontaneously occur in the process of reading, reciting, meditating, and experimenting.

Taking a journey with this book is more than reading a book of poetry or a collection of personal stories. It is a journey into the Self. I hope your journey is full of insights, laughter, and healing. Although I have written through my experiences and those with others, you are also reading about you—who you are, who you're not, and who you are growing to be. We are all spirits having a human experience, becoming more of who we were born to be, with Love centered in us as seeds.

If you desire it, this journey may reveal, remind and direct you through your next Lessons of Love.

With Love,
Darya

Chapter One.

For Unloved and Unloving Lovers & Friends

You're Just a Woman Creating Her Own Great Drama

Doing whatever you can
to impress this fine, new man—
giving up time, money, emotion—
being a therapist with relentless devotion—

You're just a woman, creating her own great drama,
giving up more than you think you oughta,
paying a price for the love of a man
who gives much less than you think he can.

Using intuition, sensing every need,
filling each one with breakneck speed,
making yourself an asset of unquestionable value—
out on a limb for a man that you hope will have you—

You're just a woman, creating her own great drama,
giving up more than you think you oughta,
paying a price for the love of a man
who gives much less than you think he can.

Now the crisis hits and you sing your song,
wailing because he neglects you all night long.
After all you do to take care of him,
attending to your needs is far from him.

You're just a woman, creating her own great drama,
giving up more than you think you oughta,
paying a price for the love of a man
who gives much less than you think he can.

When the truth is finally brought to light,
I have compassion for all who have this plight.
Still, it's part of your great dramatic tale—
to give without getting and to be left to wail.

That's why you'd pick such a man to love,
a man stuck in ICU, hanging in traction from above.
Since every part of his life is in extreme trauma,
he plays an ideal part in your creative drama.

How could he possibly nurture and attend to you,
when breathing on his own is barely all he can do.
Yet, you pay for the specialists and you pay for his "meds."
Then you run back and forth to the sides of his bed.

Any minute, you're sure he'll have a breakthrough.
Then life will balance out, and it'll be all about you!!
But what if ICU is not temporary but a pattern that's set?
What if this is life together and this is as good as it gets?

Do what you do for him because you want to do it,
or let him heal through others or by his own good wit.
Only a woman who's turned off her heart and mind,
expects more from a man in a position of this kind.

You picked the man in ICU as the object of affection,
unavailable and at war with his own life's direction.
If being his savior and healer is the road to glory,
you're making progress by co-creating this story.

At least he knew to find someone like you.
And perhaps you will discover Pure Love so true—
no hidden motives driving the things that you do—
only Pure Love radiating to others through you.

If not, just recognize the Truth:

You're just a woman creating her own great drama,
giving up more than you think you oughta,
paying a price for the love of a man
who is already giving you everything that he can!! 〰

And so I asked Spirit,
"What is Pure Love?"
This is what I was told.

Pure Love

Pure Love is not manipulation,
strings seeking to control,
nor loneliness, suffering abandonment,
orphaned in the threatening cold.

An infinite petaled flower
that graciously unfolds,
Pure Love touches the secret places
each of us holds.

Pure Love forever multiplies,
an expanding geometric progression.
It defies depletion by denials
and being boosted with false confessions.
When this world is complete,
Pure Love is its only succession.

Pure Love loves the Lover.
Returned or not, Pure Love remains.
Because within itself,
Pure Love is its own
total and complete exchange. ❈

The Power of Weakness

I was drawn by the Power of his Weakness,
growing aware of my own strengths.
I was drawn by the Power of his Weakness.
Still—my love grew great lengths.

He was drawn by the Power of my Weakness,
promises of kindness he could not resist.
He was drawn by the Power of my Weakness.
Still control—his fear of love—seemed to persist.

I found joy in knowing I could help him live.
I found meaning and power in serving love's purpose.
I received blessings of joy, freely wanting to give.
But was he my man, a project or a compelling focus?

Now I know why a mythic hero was absent in my life.
one seeming to lighten life's burdens naturally.
I carried the strong person's pain, isolation and strife,
emerging from a cocoon—alone, vulnerable and free.

The Power of Weakness draws in the Strong.
A moth to the flame, touching in, can't stay long—
unless the Strong learns to serve, love and give,
as anchoring reasons to continue to live.

Weakness appears at this Crossroads in life,
sparking courage, quickening rapid growth,
transmuting ancient fear and collective strife.
Perhaps we should take a leader's sworn oath:

Never leave our people stranded.
Always serve the ones most in need.
Walk in front, at the sides, circling to the rear.
Lead without followers. Let this be our creed.

Never feed on the Power of others' Weaknesses,
and help them see their own strengths.
Never feed on the Power of others' Weaknesses.
Share how we shift into deeper strengths.

It is the Power of my own Weakness
that inspires and pushes me.
Finding power through my helplessness
unleashes who I was born to be.

Spirit sees the Power of our Weakness,
and shows us our strengths.
Spirit sees the Power of our Weakness—
then leads us to great lengths. ☾

Next Time You Want a Woman Just for a Friend

I know transitions are rough on everyone—
the one who is leaving, the one who is left,
the one approaching, the one who is met.
It's rough to say, "Go hide until you're done,"
'Cause I know transitions are rough on everyone.

We agreed to create an illusion, to play a game:
"Let's just be friends—no blame, no shame"—
as if being friends would regulate our emotions,
or control the spiritual and physical commotion
of powerhouses united, with mutual devotion.

You run fast forward and then you retreat—
terror posing as a game of sensuality.
It's too late to try and back up now.
Can't you hear the water falling?
Love has arrived and is calling.
It's too late to ask, "What if?" or, "Whether."
Just pray we learn how to do better.

Now that we've put all this motion in the ocean,
waves of consequence are at play every day.
Go on into that backwards dance motion,
laughing and running in the opposite direction.
Face the fear again and again. Such self-deception!

Next time you want a woman just for a friend,
don't kiss her from the start,
pulling the energy up from her root,
to her crown, straight through the heart.
Learn to hold her over time.
Perhaps then, she can be your friend.

Next time you want a woman just for a friend,
don't hold her so tight and breathe her in so deep.
Don't kiss her feet so slow and so sweet.
Wait to get to know her; have no need to self-defend.
Be there for her like she is for you, if you are her friend.

Next time you want a woman just for a friend,
don't bring her to orgasm until she is limp.
She's no prostitute, and you're not her pimp.
Don't climb the mountain and run from the view.
Heal and leave her alone until you're ready to pursue.

Next time you want a woman just for a friend,
forget to hold her so tight that your bodies vibrate,
moving on her like a bull elk moves on his mate.
This is just your style when a woman is new,
so don't mark her unless she can depend on you.

Next time you want a woman just for a friend,
don't send a bird in flight through her sphere,
awakening joy and making the hurts disappear.
Just tell her you're glad to know she exists on earth,
and you'll be back some day to share your worth.

Next time you want a woman just for a friend,
remember the first times we met one another.
I was already your friend and your lover.
I was what you prayed for and came to uncover.
Denial only enlarges the truth in the end.

Next time you want a woman just for a friend,
start at the beginning with her, not at the end.
Otherwise, the deal is already done,
and you are joined at the start as one.

Next time you want a woman just for a friend,
don't call me—'cause next time I won't pretend.
In fact, next time you want a woman just for a friend,
call a man instead, and this heartache will never begin. ▼

Learn to Love the Shadow

Learn to love the shadow.
Go deeper than the shell.
If you can't love all of me,
our love's a private hell.

Love me with your heart open, and spirit free.
We can make our dreams into reality.
Time and trials may bring something else.
Meanwhile, just look for me to be myself.

Why do we fall for partners
whose ways we cannot stand?
Why don't we fall for others,
who are dying to take our hands?

I'm the same girl who caught your eye
in the middle of a crowded room.
You said my face brought tons of light.
Our eyes panned the crowd, then—zoom!

I can learn to be the one
who accepts me for who I am.
It's time to let the shining sun
meet old shadows on the run.

So, it's time to....
Learn to love the shadow.
Go deeper than the shell.
Learning to love all of me
delivers me from hell!

It makes no sense for two of us
to reject the same parts of me.
Your complaints have finally helped me
grow self-acceptability.

I said...
I can learn to be the one
who accepts me for who I am.
It's time to let the shining sun
meet old shadows on the run.

I'm loving me more and more
as I get to know myself.
So, next time a man loves me,
it's for the substance, not just the shell.

Learn to love the shadow.
Go deeper than the shell.
When I learn to love all of me,
I deliver myself from hell.

People, learn to love the shadow.
Go deeper than the shell.
Learning to love all of us
may deliver us from hell.

Face it, light it, love it, embrace it.
Learn to love the shadow.
Learn to love the shadow. 〰

There's No Such Thing as Casual Sex

There's no such thing as casual sex,
exchanging body fluids and DNA,
and maybe making lives in the mix,
sharing what's been and what might be,
with all our partners' sexual histories—
There's no such thing as casual sex.

In my thirties, something called a halt
to a secret wild woman I expressed to a fault.
It wasn't fear of syphilis or gonorrhea,
or hell that stopped this sexual diarrhea.
It was fear of Herpes, and then HIV-AIDS
that made me into a celibate renegade.

I acted as if I had convinced myself
that casual sex was required for my health.
After all, it made me feel soft and free,
defying conventions confining to me.
I felt wild, powerful and beautiful to see,
like a Goddess poised as an ancient tree.

It wasn't really that I had raging hormones,
making me give strangers a ride on my bones.
It was a need I had to do something daring,
or a desire to be held, even with no caring.
Sometimes it was a need to have revenge
for unfaithful acts of my spouse or boyfriend.

It was wondering whether I could draw any man
  with or without desire or a specific plan—
No caring about the ways I would be perceived,
  because after the fun, I could easily leave.
No clinging and yearning to make lust into love.
No begging forgiveness from the powers above.

Today, "casual sex" is often a casualty,
  like dying from foul play or accidentally.
We can find other ways to get a good workout,
  have a wild adventure or do a "payback pout."
Whether you do it for pleasure or just to fit in,
  so-called casual sex can bring life to an end.

Beyond our concerns for life and death,
sex is primal, sacred and can be good for health.
We share essential substance and lineage too,
with ancestors and descendants marching through.
Whether hearts are engaged, essence comes through.
And that's why—from a higher, neutral view—
  it's common sense and ancient wisdom too—
  There is no such thing as casual sex. 💣

I Made the Choice

Coming apart hurts,
while life goes on too soon,
not waiting for us to heal
open, gaping wounds.

I made the choice to be open with a few,
to protect, nurture, and somehow
pay my work world dues.

I drew a circle around us, surviving the break—
so we could grieve, heal, grow and
mend our broken trust.

I made the choice of how to deal out there,
beyond our circle's known
and loving care.

I made the choice to scan the public lot,
scanning the surface, then peering
beneath mantles and shields.

I made the choice to cover my breadth and depth,
showing a narrow surface, then plugging
my heart's leaking holes.

I made the choice of warding off
real intimacy, scattering me
across the fertile field.

Weary from my travels, taking me
constantly into others' zones,
I then made the choice
to call myself home.

I made the choice to love all my parts,
tattered and tender, known and unknown—
into a vibrant heart
the circle of life
has sown.

Is She Your Friend?

Is she your friend?
I was wondering because
I saw the look on her face
when you walked into the place,
a smile covering aged resentment and gloom.

Is she your friend?
I was wondering because
she's always talking badly about you,
tearing down to others the good that you do,
wanting herself to seem more important in the end.

I know you think she's your best mate,
because you travel, work and make play dates.
But someone should give you a heads up—
She rides along to cash in on your luck,
and expects you to fix what she's messed up.

When you do your thing, she looks threatened
like a person facing her most dreaded weapon.
When you step on her toes, she screams and explodes,
claiming you blocked Success from her road.
When you pursue a treasured vision or dream,
it's your fault her dream's not yet redeemed.

True friends celebrate you with joy,
sharing good times when you have a new toy.
Friends are the family we remember choosing,
counted as blessings when all else we're loosing.
Friends circle 'round to hold us in their care,
reaching across distance to show they are there.

Helping our friends is like helping ourselves,
making it fun to share when we're doing well.
Stepping in like a mother, father, sister or brother,
friends assist, giving a lift to one another.
Growing friends takes time, attention, care and
loving who we all are when we're stripped bare.

Is she your friend?
I was wondering because
you've known the loyalty of true friends,
who have worked troubles through to the end,
building support troops for whatever life sends.

So I wonder how you came to be so confused
and what lessons you need to learn about abuse.
I wonder what you thought you saw in her
that was within you, waiting to be discovered.
I wonder when you'll wake up and realize
this friendship is something you've fantasized.

That's why I was wondering—
is she your friend? ❖

Reflections:

They Find the Sweetest One

They find The Sweetest One,
who will never break their hearts.
They find the one gentle and kind,
who may endure abusive darts.

They find The Sweetest One,
who has an understanding heart.
The Sweetest One knows forgiveness,
allowing love many fresh starts.

Watch close, for The Sweetest One,
who's not the weakest one, surprises.
Predator and prey are not playing
by rules the hunter first surmises. ☪

Players and the Played

Players can't be real,
for all of life is a game.
The whole world is the same.
Just make the Play, know the steal,
keep your cover and work the deal.

I knew a Player once,
and touched him deep inside,
I felt the secret places where the real person hides—
icy caverns, frozen wounds, and explosions of lust—
because the Player's melting heart always foretells a bust.

Players don't promise, they only drop hints—
crumbs of hope for the hungry and self-convinced,
always a future meal, never the present tense.
Players paint pictures that the Played want to see
and the Played give up gold for the possibilities.

Players can't be real,
for all of life is a game.
The whole world is the same.
Just make the Play, know the steal,
keep your cover and work the deal.

Who's playing whom, the Player or the Played?
We're all in our own Play for some possibility.
Go beyond lies, truths, and accountability.
See people browsing for better probability.
But games leave someone hanging, inevitably.

Players, Players it is time to realize
you're not in control where the Spirit presides.
When Spirit locks two flames across all time,
"wannabe" controllers are due for a surprise.
The Players are the Played, a word to the wise!

Players can't be real,
for all of life is a game.
The whole world is the same.
Just make the Play, know the steal,
keep your cover and work the deal.

Players have to be smart, able to see the deal:
know what's at stake; and how much they can steal.
Prowess is their inheritance. Prowess is their wealth.
When the heart lacks courage, the mind brings stealth.
Just get the goods, and at any cost, protect the self.

Once I knew a Player who also cared for others.
Still, he wanted to play his game and not be discovered.
"Tell them who you are. Present some truth they can see.
Then let the Played have their version of reality.
The Play is an even exchange of free-will energy."

Players can't be real,
for all of life is a game.
The whole world is the same.
Just make the Play, know the steal,
keep your cover and work the deal.

Anyone who is Played has the chance to learn
what's real, what's fake, and the difference to discern.
Without the Player's masterful illusory games,
the Played would never this distinction gain.
Because of the Play, the Soul's wisdom remains.

Looking through the lens of this view of truth,
Players and the Played all come home to roost.
No more Victims to save or Persecutors to hang—
just vision for us to see and courage for us to stand,
interwoven hearts lighting paths across the land.

So just remember, people:
when we think our Play is on,
Great Spirit is playing us all,
and the game's already won. ᵚ

Don't Lie to Me

Don't lie to me; lie to someone who can't see.
Lie to strangers or when there's no intimacy.
When I discover lies from those I trust most,
they become enemies I mistakenly brought close.

I made a pact with Truth for the work that I do.
Truth comes naked, free and at the time it's due.
Lies slash and tear at the fabric of love we made,
painfully cutting deep ties with a dull sling blade.

When I am still, neutral and willing to receive,
Truth comes gently, showing me what to believe.
Whispers from others with agendas to achieve,
are silent in truth's womb, unable to conceive.

Don't lie to me; lie to someone who can't see.
Lie to strangers or when there's no intimacy.
When I discover lies from those I trust most,
they become enemies I mistakenly brought close.

From truth we may grow a choice to part as two,
while lies grow an abyss all of us fall through.
Lies breed contempt, repulsion and disdain
for the liar, who looks for others to blame.

We feed lies to love, making the sacred profane.
Our trust disappears, seeming to be in vain.
You and I shared lies slowly killing unity,
destroying our self-respect and integrity.

Don't lie to me; lie to someone who can't see.
Lie to strangers or when there's no intimacy.
When I discover lies from those I trust most,
they become enemies I mistakenly brought close.

Lies have different tones than the tones of Truth.
Even painful truths have rich tones that soothe.
I restored self-respect and integrity, and
made a pact so that Truth comes freely to me.

So, don't lie to me; lie to someone who can't see.
Lie to strangers or when there's no intimacy.

Prisoner of the Past

A Prisoner of the Past sees no way out.
He turns toward love's promise of warm sunlight.
Raising his fists to fight back with might,
he scores imagined knockouts against the Light.
Determined that being doomed in love is his plight,
he faces dark walls and he dialogues with doubt.

Wait! The death sentence has been appealed!
Someone finally loves you just as you are.
Open your heart's door and take the deal!
It's Pure Love, beyond fear, just be for real!
"No way, go away. Don't touch me where I feel!"
Later, he protests when the deal's been repealed.

It is he who sentences Love to Death,
and imprisons himself to live, as a result,
in a cell dedicated to a love-coward's cult.
The key is in the door, yet he crouches on the floor,
stuck in a prison of his story's own making,
longing for love, full of fear and heart aching.

A Prisoner of the Past sees no way out.
He turns toward love's promise of warm sunlight.
Raising his fists to fight back with might,
he scores imagined knockouts against the Light.
Determined that being doomed in love is his plight,
he faces dark walls and dialogues with doubt.

"I kill what I fear," he considerately warns!
"Wake up if you want me! Heed this alarm!
Bar the doors and lock the cell!
I long for solitary's peaceful hell.
Stay away, if you want to stay well!
I swear this is the simple truth I tell.

"So, enter at your own risk—
Step over the bones, if you please,
bones belonging to love's refugees.
Boldly, they entered this dragon's cave,
then died, consumed by raging flames."

I was a burning woman, consumed by the fire,
tempering my metals, emptying all desire.
I lived through initiations, renewed and rewired.

Now, I stand outside the Prisoner's bolted cell,
holding a sunlit sign with a message to tell.
"Prisoner of the Past, you've got it confused.
Pure Love's dew rests upon the grass that is you.
Whether it seeps through layers, depends on you—
Will you love yourself, then another, pure and true?" ☾☼≋

◇◇

Reflections:

The System May or May Not Love You Back

In every trial and challenge, find a way to success.
Go the extra mile, hustling to ace every test.
Give your all to the System, showing your worth.
The System may or may not Love you back.

So it is more than money, it is respect that's due,
appreciation, validation and warmth for you.
Some admire you while others freely attack,
and the System may or may not Love you back.

Are you looking for Love you deserve or missed?
Were you a star in some other place, not this?
If the System's cultural code is what you crack,
the System may or may not Love you back.

Systems hire change agents and others like you
to bring helpful gifts and catalytic views.
Still, they unconsciously resist and persist.
The System may or may not Love you back.

Pure Love values people whole, as they are,
unique constellations of brilliant stars—
If Love helps show more of who you really are,
the System may or may not Love you back.

The System may show its appreciation
with money, thanks or celebrations.
Others may bask in System rewards
while you watch, wishing for applause.

Are you looking for Love you deserve or missed?
Were you a star in some other place, not this?
If the System's cultural code is what you crack,
the System may or may not Love you back.

Do you give the System what it wants
and rarely get what you say you need?
Systems have special crops they grow,
to offer those they value good feed.

Systems may resist rotating crops,
although old ways make performance drop,
wanting all to conform to what they're doing,
even blocking goals they say they're pursuing.

Is there fine print in your System agreement,
saying, "Do these tasks and receive this payment?
No promise of love and emotional support,
no promise of you and the System having special rapport?"
The System may or may not Love you back."

So do your Calling in the System,
if you're in the center or on the fringe.
Pursue your purpose wherever you are,
The Soul may Call to places near and far.

If you deeply love the work that you do,
and work fits your Calling and Culture too—
If you and the System seek the same things,
Work is Love with matching rings.

Are you looking for the Love you deserve or missed?
Were you a star in some other place, not this?
If the System's cultural code is what you crack,
the System may or may not Love you back.

Systems assign Love to special departments
if you need and grieve after System allotments,
so look there for the Love you may deserve or missed,
because the System may or may not Love you back.

All Systems have some appreciation
for helpers in System Transformations,
even if helpers die from taking on this pact,
before the System learns to Love them back.

Take Visions as far as both of you can go,
beyond boundaries you and the System know.
Build foundations in the consciousness you sow,
birthing new Systems where wholeness can grow.

Love Systems for what is deep in their Souls,
both of you empowered to work as wholes.
If your work requires the cultural code to crack,
learn to see in the dark and how to watch your back,
whether the System does or doesn't Love you back.

Remember, your Presence is a powerful fact,
so listen for the Call and then get on track,
with Visions helping cultural codes to crack.

Leaders first have to Love themselves,
and then lead with Loving others as well—
The System may or may not learn to Love you back. ♒

The Two of Rejection

Our rejections are our protections
from what would cause us harm.
Our dreams are our projections
upon those we seek to charm.

It takes two for rejection to exist
between any pair this earth holds.
One leaves; the other stays to resist;
buried in pain, a body turning cold.

The rejected heart could decide
to stop its own slowing beat,
letting the Leaver's choice preside
over the Stayer's heart, once sweet.

Fearing rejection, some choose not to pursue
risky dreams their souls' impulses desire.
Yet, fearing rejection delivers the fear as true.
Dreamers throw water upon their own fires.

The Stayer may surrender all with open arms,
receiving Pure Love from within instead.
In the Leaver's winter wind, the Stayer's heart warms.
The Stayer moves on, making gold from lead.

For rejection to exist, it really takes two:
One to reject and the Second to agree.
Otherwise, the rejection is only half true.
The Second decides what the other half is to be.

For some, rejection enters as a thief in the night,
stealing the host's self-worth 'til it is less and less.
For others, rejection opens doors to golden light.
The host discovers inner treasures, and is blessed.

This shift seems an impossible switch,
only performed by the masterful mind,
like a priest, priestess, magician or witch.
Yet, we all have this space within, Divine.

This is one key to every cycle of liberation,
where one group pushes the other away.
Stayers' vision, Pure Love and determination
move them beyond loss and into what stays.

Freedom, Love and Wisdom cannot be taken
or removed from life once they've been born.
Rejection is but a powerful force to awaken us,
pledging allegiance to Love already sworn.

I pledge allegiance to my Source
and to my Infinite Supply—
to stand in Wisdom and in Love
bridging all below and above.

The ultimate marriage is between Spirit and you,
blessing rejection's traces, making these anew.
For when rejection misses being powered by two,
it may transmute into Love's power from a higher view. ✡

There is Love for the Unloved Lover

There is love for the Unloved Lover,
hidden deep beneath the muck and mire
of loud and hungry unfulfilled desire.

There is love for the Unloved Lover,
falling in showers of sunlight upon smooth wet skin,
looking for open doorways to empty spaces within.

There is love for the Unloved Lover,
forever seeking one, who flows with him or her,
while wondering if this flow can ever really occur.

There is love for the Unloved Lover within you and me,
making souls full of flickering sparks and creativity,
touched by the Infinite Presence our eyes don't even see.

What's that I heard an Inner Voice say?
"Stop waiting, wondering, wanting and wishing!
God brings the Love you thought you were missing!
Have the courtship, stir up the passion and say the vows.
Accept the comely and crusty, as unconditional love allows."

Appreciate your gifts.
Laugh lovingly at your flaws.
Pamper depleted places.
Warm the Wanderer's weary paws.
Inspire the hopeless failure in you.
Look at your courage. Be in awe.
Ignore your symptoms. Use medicine on the cause.
Reward the steady, practicing pupil--
the one determined to learn Love's Laws.

For whether married or single, the Unloved Lover can appear—
When one's alone, love's new, or has existed for many years.
Touch the Infinite Source. Love again has dominion, not fear.

Yes, God told me something...
There is love for the Unloved Lover in you and me.
That news makes me sing and sway with ecstasy.

Tonight Pure Love marries Genius and Feminine Fire.
Tonight I dance with the Unloved Lover in me.
A Sacred Teacher, she is. And a grateful student am I.

Reflections:

Reflections:

Chapter Two.

Tests and Testimonies of Love

Mother Root, Father Sky

She was the Mother Root to me,
the Ground of Father Sky, beneath the Sacred Tree.

She wove our daily reality,
without time or passion to pursue
other lifelong dreams she could have made true.

She dreamed first of loving family,
a new circle staying unbroken,
living up to vows and promises spoken.

She gave herself and her life to this dream,
a rock beneath Father Sky's waters and winds,
carrying wisdom for storms to break and bend.

She never let her children go free,
whether they walked the city streets,
or flew across the Earth's great seas.

She dreamed I would be different,
and learned to love and accept me as I was,
once I became a woman, living by my own laws.

I always wondered why she stayed so long
in a marriage she felt had gone wrong.
It was not my business, but they made it mine,
sharing facts and asking help from a child of nine.

Now I see how deeply she loved,
and how Love helped to shape her heart.
Now I'm careful what I wonder about,
because next comes the learning part.

She was the Mother Root to me,
the Ground of Father Sky, beneath the Sacred Tree. ♎

Did I Ever Say?

Did I ever say yours is the first face
deep crevices of my mind can remember?
Pools of dark brown eyes, soft and tender,
doorways to a warm heart and resting space?

Did I ever say how I counted on you
to be present in mind and body always,
to be steady, true and never fazed
when life's challenges claimed their due?

Reaching out, I always expected a prize,
not a trophy won in material form,
nor protection giving safety from harm,
just a love that held me with your eyes.

I knew you had hard times growing up,
I watched you drink from that bitter cup.
Because Dad was forever harder on you,
making love distant, seeming untrue.

With joy I took the benefits being a girl,
while resenting limits and man-made laws.
Crashing through, a rebel bent on a cause,
I looked to you for a clue in this world.

Childhood had few oases in deserts of gloom.
I felt like an orphaned, abandoned alien,
whose hope was in the story of Pygmalion.
I know we chose different paths to escape doom.

We were silent partners in a life of strife,
sustaining each other's existence,
separately portraying our own resistance,
layers of tension uncut by a tongue's knife:

Playing shadows all night long on the wall,
pretending to be airplanes 'til I would fall,
whispering beneath fights in the next room,
when, the next day, appearances would resume.

Mother's milk had no immunity
from dragons within and beyond our doors,
tests to discover what lay in our cores,
later making us leaders of community.

Did I ever say I wept to watch you sink,
deep into oblivion and hard to reach,
taunted by fears coming through you to teach,
using raging hormones to break our strong links?

Did I ever say I became frightened and lost,
you in Viet Nam, paying our country's costs?
I was uncool, losing all sense of inner calm,
a sea of emotions at night, I turned and tossed.

When you came home, I saw you were changing,
full of unspoken secrets and shattered nerves,
focused on family while life threw you curves.
Yet, I was relieved no longer to cry and wait,
because you were home, alive, well and safe.

Did I ever say I was proud of your lead,
determined to complete what you began,
committed to your family as a man.
struggling with how to start a new breed?

Getting your degree, being with family,
painting your art, plus all your creative starts,
showing up to share, telling others you care,
looking forever young, showing us how it's done—
I'm so proud of you. Can't you see it's true?

Sometimes it's hard for the firstborn who arrives.
Firstborns pave the way for the rest of us to drive.
They do what they have to without much fuss,
and make choices that long affect the rest of us.

On October 21st, this day of your birth
you've gone 52 times around this earth.
I hope you know how much you're worth
to all of us for whom you came first.

May your journey the next fifty-two
bring everlasting joy and victory too.
Knowing yourself is the key to win.
Then you know God, my brother and friend.

Did I ever say how much I've always loved you?
Well, believe me, dear brother, I truly do.

Six Years Later in 2005, There's Almost No One Left to Call Me "Peach"

Now it is six years later in 2005,
two years since you left us and died,
joining Mom and Dad on the other side.

There's almost no one left to call me "Peach,"
no one who knows how, when or why
I came to be what I am and what I teach.

They all crossed over early, one by one,
as if they had somewhere better to run.
And there's almost no one left to call me "Peach."

They loved me their way, I loved them mine.
I asked them for little and took to my own design.
Love's legacies remain in hearts and deeds within reach.
And there is almost no one left to call me "Peach." ♎♒

I Prayed for You to Come

Almost six, and pleased with where I fit in the mix—
The Peach of Dad's eye, I ran to him when I cried.
I loved and stood up for my big brother
while Mom shook her head and sighed—
As a child, I wasn't the daughter she had in mind.

Baby sister to a loving older brother,
I carved out a place to be smart, social and pretty.
I was adventurous, always ready to discover—
places, people and things, ideas and lucid dreams.
At home I brought help and domestic gifts,
creating food and offering us a spiritual lift.

But I must have heard your call to meet again,
and travel this time as sisters and friends.
I must have dreamed of comfort and fun,
'cause I remember I prayed for you to come.

No thoughts of losing my place,
or of having less in a children's love race—
Like people who've been asking for a change,
and not thinking of how life will rearrange.

I couldn't wait for you to come home,
where I was a secret alien and felt alone.
I could show you everything I had learned,
and protect you from dangers I had discerned.

You came early, sparking fear you might not live.
They kept you from me, concerned with care to give.
I started all over again to make my new place,
while you grew healthy through prayers and grace.

I stole moments, away from the eyes of others,
whispering to you, touching your crib's pink covers.
I sat with you under the healing powers of the sun,
making sure you knew I wouldn't leave you alone.

You made your place with beauty, wit and grace.
You were the daughter winning Mom's "Girlie Cup,"
focused on things like playing with hair and make-up.

You grew to be a source of pride for us all,
giving me reason to brag for deeds large and small.
Now you share with others everything you've learned,
a leader protecting them from dangers you've discerned.

Now we've become one another's touchstones,
elders in our family and working women, alone.
We celebrate each other and make loud applause,
for we carry our roots, their strengths and their flaws.

I must have heard your call to meet again
and travel this time as sisters and friends.
I must have dreamed of comfort and fun,
because I remember I prayed for you to come. ♑

Reflections:

Measuring the Love

Who has more and who has less?
Who gets the most and who's loved the best?
Who does the most and who has to do less?
Measuring the love to find out who's blessed.

Sense the energy in a circle and quickly see
who the circle marks for having high currency.
High currency carriers are called to feed
a system's unconscious deep layers of need.

High currency is intangible and moves invisibly,
shifting into substance matching system's needs.
Try to measure its value, you may come up short.
High currency is the Infinite Source's sport.

Who has more and who has less?
Who gets the most and who's loved the best?
Who does the most and who has to do less?
Measuring the love to find out who's blessed.

We see high currency carriers as being born with more.
Siblings ponder winning or how to even the score.
Family circles take for granted the energy received,
disturbed beyond reason when the energy leaves.

High currency carriers may seem to pay more
for illusions of love never reaching their core.
Other's sense a debt high currency carriers owe,
and demand a payment when self-esteem runs low—

As if high currency carriers are born to give
whatever others ask so that they may live.
The true gift they carry is meant to be taught—
receiving from the Source what can't be bought.

Who owes whom what and is the debt ever paid
for having more energy than others have made?
Search the Universe for karmic debts we all owe.
All currencies are called for new seeds we'll sow.

Saying those with more goodies are the ones who are blessed
pretends that others are cursed with journeys of distress.
What if their role is to wake us up to our mess,
so we balance the past and ace Pure Love tests.

Why not ask—
"Who gives more and who needs less?"
"Who serves the most and who loves the best?"
"Who teaches the most and does what Spirit requests?"

Stop measuring the love, and let our currencies confess—
We're one body moving energy to supply it where needed.
Pouring the Love passing through is the same Light we're receiving.

Pure Love is a blessing, a Spirit-to-Human-to-Spirit trade—
like blessing rains after storms cleansing the world we've made. ♦

Reflections:

Everlasting, Ever Present Love

Daughter of my body, reflection of my soul,
you're my life's treasure, you're my life's gold.
Daughter of my body, reflection of my soul,
our love is a blessing, our love is three-fold.

You are my daughter, my sister and my friend.
From the beginning, there has been no end.
For when I first held you, I learned who I was too.
We are everlasting, ever present love.

Daughter of my body, reflection of my soul,
you're my life's treasure, you're my life's gold.
Daughter of my body, reflection of my soul,
our love is a blessing, our love is three-fold.

I never knew my heart was broken,
until you came for it to open.
When I first kissed your face, new life fell into place—
Then came everlasting, ever present love.

To grow in Pure Love's ways,
it helps to remember the day
I found everlasting, ever present love.

Daughter of my body, reflection of my soul,
you're my life's treasure, you're my life's gold.
For you are everlasting, ever present love.
You are everlasting, ever present love.
You are everlasting, ever present love.

I Love You, I Worship God

I love you and I worship God.
Can we live in truth and love,
cherish and respect each other
beyond ego's tempting fraud?

I see who you are
and who you can be,
loving you inside and out,
up close and intimately.

But God is my maker—
Creator of Heaven and Earth.
Don't ask me to worship you,
for these worlds you did not birth.

Pedestals aren't for humans.
On Earth our feet can stand.
Great Mystery sparks within us
Divine Order and a greater plan.

I thank God we came together
to work and burn our raging fire.
I'll be with you in love and honor.
I'll respect what your deeds inspire.

I nestle upon your massive chest.
I hide in your comforting arms.
I melt into your swaying body,
soothed by bass tones of your charms.

Still, God is my maker,
Creator of Heaven and Earth.
Don't ask me to worship you,
for these worlds you did not birth.

I love you and I worship God.
Stay with me in Truth and Love.
Let's cherish and respect each other
beyond ego's tempting fraud.

I see who you are
and who you can be,
loving you inside and out,
up close and intimately.

I love and honor you,
and I worship God. ♥

Looking for that Mother-Father Kind o' Love

Yeah, a man is looking for that Mother kind o' Love,
that "loving-me-means-you-stay-no-matter-what-
I-do" kind o' love, that "make-a-circle-while-Daddy-
holds-the-line" kind o' love, "'cause anything else is a rub
against the claim that you really love me
like you say," meaning "you-stay-no-matter-what-
I-do-even-to-you" kind o' love.

"'Cause no matter what I do,
my 'Moms' is still my 'Moms' for true.
So what good is having one woman, not a few—
if she's not coming through, with that Mother kind o' love?"

A man's looking for that Mother kind o' love, aren't you?

A woman's looking for that Father kind o' love,
that "protect-me-from-what-would-cause-me-harm"
kind o' love, that "bring-the-energy-I-need-to-live-
while-Mama-makes-it-into-form-by-what-she-gives"
kind o' love, "'cause anything else would be a rub against
the promise that you love me like you say," meaning "you-
cherish-me-no-matter-what-I-do-even-to-myself" kind o' love.

"'Cause I can do bad my myself,
and if you're not gonna bring better health or wealth,
what good is having a man, not a child, for myself—
if he's not coming through with that Father kind o' love?"

A woman's looking for that Father kind o' love, aren't you?

Yeah, we're all looking for that Mother-Father kind o' love,
that "beyond-your-habits-roles-and-goals" kind o' love,
that "standing-in-for-present-and-absent-parts-of-parents" kind o' love,
that "testing-a-lover's-worth-based-on-needs-from-the-family-of-birth" kind o' love,
that "surrogates-for-the-powers-of-heaven-and-earth" kind o' love,
that "earth-wind-fire-water-above-and-below" kind o' love.

Everyone's looking for that Mother-Father kind o' love, aren't you?
Let's love ourselves better than we once knew how,
then love others beyond what our limits allow.
Then we are loving with that Mother-Father kind o' love.
Aren't you? ☯

The Awakening

You awaken my body and heart
from a long cryogenic sleep,
bringing morning tears to my eyes
for times I have forgotten to weep.

Your hands touch places
where I perhaps have never lived.
I melt into love's essence, captured
in sacred vessels with secrets to give.

The ground shakes beneath me.
Unsteadied, my heart opens wide.
I empty my cup, stunned and surprised.

Waves flow freely, as at evening tide.
I am relieved, for love is conceived.
Find me free in the feminine flow,
renewed by Spirit, ready to receive.

Awakenings are electrical catalytic starts.
We both have capacity for high voltage sparks.
Bring on life-changing surges. Bring on the big charge!

Excuse me—I have one burning question—
Do awakenings stick around for daily domestic parts—
providing steady wood for home fires, small and large?
I hear silence, and then…"Take one moment at a time."

Never mind. Go ahead.

Awaken my body and heart
from a long cryogenic sleep,
bringing morning tears to my eyes
for times I have forgotten to weep.

Your hands touch places
where I perhaps have never lived.
I melt into love's essence, captured
in sacred vessels with secrets to give. 〰

I Dreamed You Up

This song is for you,
who I can finally touch.
This song is for you,
who I already love so much.

If you're really real,
it's more than chance or luck.
If you're really real,
it's 'cause I dreamed you up.

I've dreamed up houses and cars,
dreamed of Venus and Mars.
I've dreamed up money and fun.
It's taken forever for you to come.

The way you move through air,
a voice so deep and so rare.
I'll drink from your cup—
Hold me. I dreamed you up.

No one has ever drawn me
like you promise to do.
Showing my soul unbarred to you,
I'm free, and you're my destiny.

I've dreamed up houses and cars,
dreamed of Venus and Mars.
I've dreamed up money and fun.
It's taken forever for you to come.

My soul's always known you'd come,
yet I've been so alone and blue,
except for the promise of you.
So, I just dreamed you up.

A man so fine and so rare;
a heart ready to share.
And now the dream is real—
flesh and bone I can feel.

I've dreamed up houses and cars,
dreamed of Venus and Mars.
I've dreamed up money and fun.
It's taken forever for you to come.

You walked right over to me.
There was no place else to be.
'Cause I dreamed you up, and
then you handed me that cup.

The way you move through air,
a voice so deep and so rare.
I'll drink from your cup—
Hold me. I dreamed you up.
We have a lot to create,
We have a lot to dream up.
Dream up. ♥

I Touched Love

I touched a miraculous space
where nothing could exist
but love, love, Pure Love
and the ecstasy of bliss.

Impatience left without a trace.
Fear's anxieties were erased.
Only love, love, Pure Love could exist.
No other could survive or resist.

I rode full moon's midnight ecstasy,
touched an ancient choir's geometry.
Sacred shapes of God's Creation
rippled through my body's sea.

I wanted to tell everyone
what this meant and why.
My words were much too small
to paint the vast blue sky.

So I bathed in Love's powders,
and hummed its melodic touch.
I put my tears in its rapid waters,
braving its intense clutch.

In the mirror's soft reflection,
physically I was not the same.
Touching Love transfigured me
in the fires of its violet flames.

Come, touch Love with me today,
our hands and hearts in its fire.
Streams of light thread through us all.
Creation's web is Love, beyond desire.

What Made Me Love You?

Was it wisdom walking all over your face,
Spirit's army marching as you entered a space?
Was it light beaming brightly when you prayed,
a mouth speaking sounds from Spirit's pathways?
Was it these things that made me love you?

I admit, these things made me swoon,
heartstrings tied to an invisible balloon.
My hips swayed to drums while my heart flew,
and we sang old love songs we both knew.
Yet, from this love did not spring.

Was it memory of our love ages ago,
more than recalling lost love and its pain?
Was it my heart's unfulfilled desire
reaching for a past unrealized gain?
Was it these things that made me love you?

These created powerful bonds, like a chain,
a pact that we'd meet again and again,
on fields of friendship and in courts of love,
with a sense of union flowing from above.
Yet, for all this I did not claim to love.

Was it the danger of threats I sensed
from all directions, past and present tense,
knowing somehow I was destined to fall
unless I said "No" to Spirit's beckon and call?
Was it these things that made me love you?

No, these made life an intense adventure,
a journey to take and be remembered,
perhaps for despair, perhaps for rapture,
with inner prizes we both would capture.
For this I called on my will, not Pure Love.

Was it the frailty of a man in grief,
tortured by worlds of past pain and emotion,
masked in all the roles you felt compelled to keep,
hoping to hide from sight the terror underneath?
This touched my heart. It made me weep.

It was all these things that made me find
the Pure Love I had deep inside.
The love I felt went beyond me and you,
to a treasured inheritance come due:

Electro-magnetics between us like I've never known,
a foundation we were building for what Spirit had sown,
the way we laughed from our depths and spoke in code,
no matter who was around, we could be alone.
The way you rushed to fill me in about times past,
warning that love may not come, or be long to last,
the way you took care to keep me as a friend,
gently learning about me, seeking not to offend.

Loving you made me carry my own water.
You were not here, so I chopped my own wood.
Loving you brought me to Pure Love for a man.
I burned my own fire, spoke truth, took a stand.

Loving you was a gateway to a paradise I could not see,
sparking a vast explosion on the other side of me.
Loving you took me there and pushed me off a cliff.
Falling with lightning speed, I found wings to lift.
Swans fly straight through lightened hearts,
showing Love's shadows once standing apart.
Exiled for ages from this Love of mine,
shadows waited for birth of Pure Love, Divine.

Loving you opened the heart of me
to golden rays of Love for all eternity.

And, that is what made me love you. ♦

Who, but You?

Who, but you could have taken me here,
could hold the energy so fiercely,
and not even open your ears?

Who, but you could resist heartbroken sounds,
then walk away and not turn around
to heal ancient wounded ground?

I know they call you the Ice Man,
and I know you are loving too.
I know you had a job to do, and
I must have picked you for it too!

Who, but you could enter my heart so deep,
engaging me with your passions and trials,
and reach my dreams as I sleep?

Who, but you could have taken me by surprise,
stealing me by day, with your closed eyes,
and my head turned up to the skies?

I looked around, and I was on the ground.
I was flying high, and then I fell down.
Not truly—but old movies in my mind
showed such images, feelings and sounds.

Spirit had to remind me of the lessons—
"Relationships are perfect mirrors, you know.
He has held the energy for you to unfold
the whole of who you are, ever evolving star.
Homeward come all your exiled parts,
no matter the outcomes, no matter the starts."

Who, but you could trigger these deep lessons
of inner mysteries and power as blessings,
fruit of Pure Love's true confessions?

Who, but you could remind me I am Pure Love so true?
Thank you, Dear One, for in this lesson
I am now resting. ❊

Come to Me at the First Snow

When the sky is indigo
and the moon is new,
when hunters have counted coup,
come to me at the first snow.

When time's pendulum is still
and ambivalence is nil,
when love's bonded with will,
come to me at the first snow.

Drive along my winding road.
Walk the way the elk herd goes.
Fly the way the eagles know, but
come to me at the first snow.

When the North Star is aglow
and our miracle has sparked,
when Love is sealed between our hearts,
come to me at the first snow.

Gone are obstacles from before.
Pure intentions connect our core.
Come because Spirit told you so.
Come to me at the first snow.

Like swans, geese and the cedar trees,
perhaps we love eternally.
I only ask you to promise me—
Come to me my darling.
Come to me at the first snow. ☾

Feathers Fly Away

Once words are clearly spoken,
hearts may be healed or broken.
Like feathers blowing in high wind
words may not be retrieved again.
Words spoken, like feathers, fly away.

Words may fly like whirling winds,
opening wounds from deep within.
When our words have flown away,
they leave marks and tracks that stay.
Words spoken, like feathers, fly away.

No matter what we send out,
all comes back to us, no doubt.
We can make it just as much fun
to receive what we've begun.
Words spoken, like feathers, fly away.

Dad said "Think before you speak.
Gain success in what you seek."
Whatever my heart intends
should go with the words I send.
Words spoken, like feathers, fly away.

Reach out to heal and mend
whatever you've done to offend.
Extend your heart and hand,
never repeat the wound again.
Words spoken, like feathers, fly away.

Speak to me true Love's words.
Hearts testifying truth are heard.
We'll fly with eagles to the sun.
We'll bring back the Love we've won.
Words spoken, like feathers, fly away.

Let's use words to help uplift,
we don't know who gets the gift.
Feathers blowing in high wind
may bless many in the end.
Words spoken, like feathers, fly away. ✈

When My People Love You

When my people love you, you know you've been loved.
We spare no affection, we hold back no applause.

When my people love you, be all of who you are.
Show us your differences, the shape of your star.

When my people love you, you know how love feels.
We help you keep on going, if you're keepin' it real.

When my people love you, it's 'cause you stand up for us,
making loads feel lighter, building hope and trust.

When my people love you, it's 'cause you see our needs.
When you get the spotlight, show the world where we bleed.

When my people love you, it's 'cause you love us free,
showing us co-creation and inequities.

We wrap you in blankets and care.
We guide you with wisdom and prayers.
We touch you with deep belly laughs.
We blow minds with creativity and crafts.

Businesses capitalize on what we create,
using rhythmic sayings in ads as bait.
But when we work within corporate walls,
they act like our flavors don't sell at all.

We push self and others with our truths.
We move our bodies to keep things loose.
We soothe wounds with rich voices and hugs.
We even give strangers rhythm and love.

We watch others copy what we create,
when we can't seem to get through the gate.
We draw from our souls to raise good fruit,
and yearn to remember our ancient roots.

When my people love you, go 'head, love us back.
We're all related—and before light there was black. ○

I Love This Land and This Land Loves Me

Lush green ferns surround the paths of my feet,
rolling fields, cool forests, high canopies of trees,
old immortal ones nurse the future trees to be—
 I love this land and this land loves me.

Twin fawns are born and take their first steps,
elk herds bathe in the sun, building their health,
coyotes yip while others fall to their deaths—
 I love this land and this land loves me.

Plant medicine grows strong, shows me what I need,
huge rocks support me, healing wounds that bleed,
cross-winds gather to plant the future's seeds—
 I love this land and this land loves me.

Nights of star-crowded skies within my arm's reach,
dreams and visions come to inform what I teach,
a man joins me in Love, and comes to call me Peach—
 I love this land and this land loves me.

Infinite space to unfold my entire energy field,
I co-create with others new forms to be revealed,
falling waters help us to make our dreams real—
 I love this land and this land loves me.

I fight for this land and for the lives that run free,
honor the blood of ancients here and across the sea.
Spirit pointed the way here through visions I could see,
 drawing me cross-country for creativity.

I drowned in raging waters and I burned in desert fires,
climbed jagged mountains and slipped on traps of desire.
Tossed in turbulent winds, I practiced the willow's bend.
Pummeled with hail stones, I stood with Spirit, not alone.

These are good and small things to pay to live this way.
For I come from lines of people stolen from land, histories broken.
I come from many lands stolen from people whose stories are spoken.
I come from many directions, here and far away,
building health, union and visions of future days.

You ask me what I'm doing and why I'm living here.
I wonder myself and then recall a vision so clear.
I am birthing a Vision and a Vision is birthing me.
So don't ask me as if there's someplace else I need to be.
I love this land, and this land loves me. ♦〰

◇◇◇

Reflections:

Reflections:

Reflections:

Chapter Three.

At Last, Heal the Past

Four Love Quests

What is the wound that has never fully healed?
What is the great lie and the truth the lie concealed?
What is the urgent dream that must be made real?
What is the part of you yearning most to be revealed?

Unleash Pure Love stored beneath the heart's great seal.
Circulate Pure Love within. Use all your zeal. 〰●◆

No One Remembers, No One Tells

Remember, each family is like a nation
in a child's reality and imagination.
No one remembers and no one tells
national secrets patriots know too well.
Fear constructs silent monuments of doubt,
with red flags against telling or you'll be cast out.

The need for love revises the grief and pain,
and patriots are prisoners, protesting in vain.
Daily life goes on, appearances being mundane.
There are no safe places in this dangerous domain.
Wounds go untreated, beneath bandages and waste.
Little patriots dream and plan for future escapes.

No one remembers, no one tells
national secrets patriots know too well.
Molesters are traitors who invade their own troops, and
respond as if betrayed when all comes home to roost.
Perpetrators persist, imagining their deeds go unseen,
while we live on a universal projection screen.

Memories become triggered sensations,
without full meaning or true explanations,
justifying emotional and physical defenses, like
toughness and strength, belying frightened tenderness.
As adults, little patriots struggle to connect the dots,
co-creating lives with betrayal and exploitation plots.
Fear, hurt and low self-worth are the causal roots
of occupational dramas and low integrity pursuits.

No one remembers, no one tells
national secrets patriots know too well—
Until one day, we meet the right catalytic force,
turning memory's sensations into flashes of light,
showing the course of relations repeating these plights.

Then someone remembers, someone tells,
helping our lineages heal and begin to live well.
For there are no dark places that go forever unseen,
while we live on a universal projection screen.

So, now we remember and now we tell.
Now we forgive ourselves and others as well.
We restore our self-worth and remove our armor,
no longer drawing perpetrators to replay these traumas.

Now we remember and now we tell.
Now we start over, learning to love ourselves.
We start by remembering why we were truly born,
what we agreed to do this time and the promises sworn.

We remember that Creation is before the womb.
Active Intelligence never dies, or stays in a tomb.
We remember that any wound received can be healed.
We're light arranged in flesh, branded with Creator's Seal.

Learning to love the self is a worthy pursuit.
Survivors thrive in new soil, growing new roots.

The Wound that Wants to be Healed

I jumped out of bed one morning, shocked and surprised,
that I was drawn to you, in part, by wounds in disguise.
We lived with frequent violence in our home spaces,
distrusting our protectors, and suffering disgraces.

When a protector begins to violate a small child,
home becomes a danger zone—small but wild.
Violations may be beatings, verbal attacks, molestations.
I recalled the beatings and hid the rest from recollection.

It's one thing to play sex games between consenting adults,
who both had sexual abuse in unsafe families or church cults.
It's another matter for adults to secretly amuse themselves,
touching a child's genitals, wounding the child's safe self.

I never acknowledged flashes of memory made plain
of Dad using me as part of some erotic game.
Others have experienced much worse trauma.
After a year, Dad stopped this abusive drama.

Violation and ambivalence were already set,
buried beneath a strong will to escape this mess,
a child fighting advances of boys and men,
never living in peace, having to self defend.

All of a sudden, I understood a base attraction to you,
why I draw and resist men with ambivalent pursuits.
This is why I wore layers to protect me from harm,
why dangerous men once drew me with their charm.

Now, I see how you protected me from yourself,
and shared generously with me your kinds of wealth.
Now, my compassion grows for all the Wounded Ones,
Abused and Abusers, healing from deeds that were done.

Spirit sent you to me soon before Dad crossed over,
passing you the torch to show my wounds still covered.
My pain wasn't about you, but about the theft I sensed.
Something had been stolen, and I looked for what I'd missed:

A voice that could speak out, so firm and strong, saying
"Don't treat me this way. What you are doing is wrong."
A child's abuse sparks the heroic adult's pursuits.
Heal the old wound, claim your power and speak the truth.

As Mothers and Older Sisters, Fathers and Older Sons,
we protect those in our care, breaking lines of despair.
We do what it takes not to repeat the same mistakes,
making a new inheritance for future generations' sakes.

We are vigilant in dark spaces where our children live,
exposing abuse from outside and also from within.
Breaking the silence, we no longer birth and breed
minds repeating tyranny's violating deeds.
Speaking the truth and facing our piercing wounds—
We are worthy heroes and heroines, awaking
to our callings, rising from hidden tombs.

Step by step, we climb out of the dark abyss,
learning to love ourselves in ways we've missed. ❀

Child of Love's Hope

I thought the moment was finally here
when you, as a parent, would show quite clear
how to love a child you claim to hold dear.

Until that moment I never even knew—
What I yearned for as a present from you
was my own version of Pure Love so true.

I did not know the difference between
love ties that bind those of blood family
and the nature of Love, purely conceived.

Families are bound by branches of hope's seeds,
yearning to give or receive what meets our needs,
speaking love's words we want to hear and believe.

I wished for a protection that was never there.
I reached for a rock. I found mostly thin air.
A moment of Love's testimony from you
was instead the moment I owed to myself,
a reckoning of debts, Self-Love overdue.

So I chose a path supporting myself,
and told you my fresh unheard truth.
"I thought you were speaking of loving me—
to find you were concerned mostly for you."

"Peach, would you give me $10,000 to repay my Aunt?"
Not working for a year, I said, "That wouldn't be smart.
But you could sell the house, and get ready cash,
buy a smaller condo and the stress would pass.
I'm already stretched with no income and debts overdue."

I waited to hear an understanding response from you.
I thought you were saying "Well, the last thing I'd want to do
is ask for something that would bring harm to you—
because I love you too much, and that wouldn't do."
Instead what you said was "Well, the last thing I'd want to do
is ask for something that would bring harm to you—
because I may need you later, and that wouldn't do."

I checked my hearing and asked you gently to repeat—
Driving sounds could cause words like "love" to delete.
But I heard you right and true, being concerned mostly for you.
You were loving me your way, and we all love like we do.

I wished for a protection that was never there.
I reached for a rock. I found mostly thin air.
A moment of Love's testimony from you
was instead the moment I owed to myself,
a reckoning of debts, Self-Love overdue.

So I chose a path supporting myself
and I told you my fresh unspoken truth.
"I thought you were speaking of loving me—
to find you were concerned mostly for you."

Silence filled the car and I listened with my heart.
I heard surprise and felt a connection so dear.
You said, "On one thing I can always count—
When you speak your mind so firm and clear,
it's always something that I need to hear."

I know this truth was not the love I hoped was due.
I know you expected to hear a plain "Yes" on cue.
But when I purify the scene with the color of blue,
emerging into view are inner children of us two:
yours, seeing love as being provided for, and
mine accepting love as not being asked for more.

When I saw our money struggle as a small child,
I loved by asking for nothing and going the extra mile.
I did what I could to fill in the gaps I saw,
as if I had more currency than others were allowed,
when it came to my needs, keeping my head bowed.

As a child, you missed being provided for,
moving through a world of revolving doors.
You learned to work the "haves" to get needs met.
What they had to give, you were ready to accept,
and others faced the short and long-term effects.

For each of us, love had distorted meaning,
shaped by survival of what we were missing.

Now in this new moment,
I accept our different ways of loving,
and how love's currency was spent.

Now I tap my roots deeply,
pulling Love from within.
Child of Love's Hope,
parent the self.
Be born again. ▼

I Want to be a Better "Man" than My Daddy Was

I flourished in mixed messages as a 50's/60's girl.
Trailblazing women made space for us in this world.
Men have an inner female and women, an inner male.
Each has centuries of privilege and oppression to unveil.
Each family is a nation where we can learn and grow—
Learn to love who you are and how to work as a whole.
So, one day in our nation, I signed up for a cause:
"I want to be a better 'man' than by Daddy was."

"Don't sit that way!" "Don't play that masculine game."
"Let the boys win a competition! Hold back, refrain."
"Learn to sew and cook." "Keep yourself pretty and clean."
"No marks on your body." "Keep wounds inside, unseen."

"It's great to be smart! Always study and achieve!"
"Do your best, but not too well, or your man will leave."
"Love hard. Give your all." "Fight well." "Always be strong."
"The wait for a dependable man can be much too long."

After programming a Black girl to make it by herself,
everyone still expected her to marry—and marry quite well.
But I didn't know what it meant to count on a man
without being disappointed, and left alone to stand.

I came to expect certain things from counting on Dad:
broken promises, deserted dreams and feeling sad,
the shame of drunkenness and the constancy of grief,
comforting him in his sorrow, so I could get relief.

After seeing him break his word for the millionth time,
I sobbed, losing a dreamed-of-father who was never mine.
Then, I reclaimed my hopes and chose myself a new cause,
deciding, "I want to be a better man than my Daddy was."

I didn't know 'bout Carl Jung and depth psychology stuff.
I looked for a way out of not feeling good enough.
Yes, all of us do the best we can at any given time in life.
Dad was no exception in how he coped with his own strife.

Still.........

I wanted to keep my word to others, give myself what I need.
I wanted to be a parent a child can trust to love and lead.
Being a girl was great, but girls didn't seem to make the laws.
That's why I wanted to be a better "man" than my Daddy was.

Now, I'm glad I spent time growing the driving inner male,
and growing feminine power on earth and beyond the veil.
As we enter a time when Feminine Laws are coming forth,
I celebrate being born to help us all find our true worth.

My Inner Voice roars—

"Seek wisdom of all life, and those who came before,
to help make your own strides, and open new doors.
What each generation faces in its own time,
boosts the next spiral forward, showing you signs."

It's a sacred declaration for living populations,
each generation charged to advance all relations—
signed up for the cause of all people's liberation
saying, "I want to be a better man than my Daddy was." ♦

You' de' Medicine Man

Ev'rybody's got somethin' to heal,
with the loved ones they draw in.
So, get the lessons, take the medicines,
and risk going for the true, real deal.

Some doctor tricks stir wounds and dreams
from times forgotten, and never healed,
Takin' tricky medicine can help reveal
gifts your spirit's yearnin' to redeem.

Some doctors have that easy medicine,
a Dr. Feelgood kind of blessing,
where Love flows like waves cresting,
and after healin' there's peaceful resting.

Tricky medicine brought me to my knees,
prayin' the healin' would end real quick.
I screamed "Okay, okay, I got it!",
tryin' to talk away my dis-ease.

I recall prayin' for true love to come,
so I must've needed the lesson,
leadin' to takin' tricky medicine,
hittin' me like lightnin' from above.

Power is the medicine we're all makin'
from the medicines we're all takin'.
We're all born with gifts to be wakin',
to use, and not be forsakin'.

'Cause I faced the roots of what I feel,
who I am wants to be revealed,
claimin' my power, I see the deal—
What's that I hear?
"Love has equal space with Power
in Pure Love's Infinite Flower."

And that's why I say—
"You' de' Medicine Man for sure,
so don't you worry 'bout me.
I was sick, you came to treat me,
so I could take the total cure."
Then, Dr. Feelgood came for sure. ℞ ☯

Reflections:

The Heart of a Babe Hidden

When the spirit of a young brown girl
with beaming eyes and a laughing smile
touches your heart with an open hand,
and your wounds and grief are beguiled—

When she asks you, "How can I assist?"—
Think of me and start to understand,
there's no hidden agenda or plan.
She's sharing Pure Love from her heart,
giving to you, a familiar man.

There is nothing you must pay her,
no bill arrives marked past due.
Accepting what she has to offer,
You are learning to accept me too.

If she calls you with a burning need,
asking for help with a passing trial,
you're in her circle to give and receive,
where Love's deeds flow as the River Nile.

There's no string attached to her prayers,
no voodoo she's hiding from your view,
When you answer her cries for help,
you have learned to assist me too.

For every offer you accept today,
for every service you freely offer,
when you think of me this way,
gold enters the heart's coffers.

With genuine thoughts of best wishes
coming straight from your heart my way,
you touch the tapestry of relations
where our joined souls happily once laid.

The heart of a babe was once hidden
in the body of this woman, shaken
by love that opened her to the core,
before confusion and closed doors.

The heart of a babe brings words spoken
from the body of this woman, shaken,
helping her find new life on firm ground,
while she twists in Creation's next round.

The heart of a babe becomes open,
in this changed woman, once shaken,
flying free to the fires of the sun,
tucked in the wings of an ancient bird.
She lands wherever she is needed,
as she's called by the Sacred Word.

Listen close to the heart of a babe,
one hidden or open to be taken.
The sound may be what awakens
the babe's heart once hidden in you,
now opening and healing, 'til the end
this time, from some long ago aching.

Love the Heart of a Tyrant

When you can love the heart of a Tyrant—
the obsessed, controlling woman or man—
The Wounded One's heart heals within us all.
Secrets of the Compassionate Ones
lie in the palms of your hand.

Stand up for your rights,
and those of all humanity.
Recognize your ancestral place
in the Universe's Geometry,—
a diamond web of creation,
flowing through all reality—
the double pyramid, circle
and helix of life's continuity.

Reach out to the heart of a Tyrant,
where ego restricts the flow of life.
Reach out to the heart of a Tyrant.
Be a Conductor of Electrical Light.

Love's holy ground appears figural,
clarifying your focus and sight. ✠

Love Thine Inner Me

The domain of the Spiritual Warrior is within.
To fathom the self is the stealth fighter's win.
Riches found are not the other's to rescind, so
the Invisible proves to be the Infinite Source again.

Examine the guidance to love one's enemy,
and to love thy neighbor as thyself.
Should the oppressed put these instructions to the test?
If so, who will be blessed?

At first, it seems to be guidance that is designed
as an opiate for otherwise intelligent minds.
Invaders cannot succeed where you abide
unless your hands and minds are bound and tied.

"Love thine enemy" has been used to control
peoples, nations, and the inheritance they hold.
I looked for deeper meaning in the ground of old.
I asked Spirit, and here is what I was told:

Jesus' words tapped power the powerless could seize,
directing people to the power within first,
an endless legacy.

Not only is this a path to one's spiritual wealth,
it is a way to your God
and Highest Self.

When waging war in the external world,
look inside first for a reflective view.
Slow down the attack, give your mirror a whirl,
and witness the Inner Me and its truth:

Loving one's enemy captures
the enemy inside as you,
an intimate connection,
not a separate truth.

When embracing a deep inner view,
outer perspectives may appear anew.
"How am I like what I despise and admire in you?
How am I stingy or greedy,
if not for wealth, but for some other revenue?
What are the deeper motives and needs
making all of this true?"

Loving the Inner Me shines the light fully inside,
giving the energy to heal whatever resides.
As the light grows inside, more power presides.
In your presence, enemies see themselves too.
The lever to transform is deep inside,
and it is powered by you.

Love Thine Inner Me—
not for the sake of the enemy,
but for the sake of the enemy
within you. ♥ ☦ ☪ ✡ ☯ ♦

Paint Me the Color of Love

Paint me the Color of Love, my God,
across the canvas of all my wounds.
Paint me the Color of Love, my God;
restore my heart where it was ruined.

Paint us the Color of Truth, my God.
Paint us right where we once stood.
I want to know what comes through,
when all's been purified in blue.

Paint me the Color of Love, my God.
Paint my mind's inner eye.
I want to see what Creator sees
in green grass and deep blue sky.

Paint me the Color of Love, my God.
Paint me the Color of Truth.
I'll show truth across all times,
and I'll live by Pure Love's Laws.

Paint me the Color of Love, my God.
Paint me the Color of Truth.
I'll journey from beginning to end,
and build a bridge of rainbow hues.

Paint me the Color of Love, my God.
Paint me the Color of Truth.
Renew me in waters behind the sun,
and virgin pathways I'll pursue.

Paint me the Color of Love, my God.
Paint me the Color of Truth.
Every inch of this brand new life
is now unquestionable proof. ♥

Faith in Love

I burn refusals in yellow-orange fire,
no longer kindling unmet desire.

Burn refusals in yellow-orange fire.
No longer kindle unmet desire.

No longer wish, weep or wail
for promises not kept,
and vows never made,
no tears for what we designed
to suffer, die or fail.

Pure Love lifts us all to fly free
from old limits, defying destiny.
So, take love's dreams off death row.
Have "faith and works" for what remains Unknown,
with these as seeds for what shows and grows.

Faith in Love lives through war and peace.
Faith in Love lives on—
expressed by you and me. ♐

A Love Equation

We do not receive more love than
we love our own authentic selves,
for no matter how another loves us,
what we receive matches the inner self.

The lodestone is the Lover within,
magnetizing Love's radiant wealth.
To know the mysterious nature
of the Inner Lover's hidden treasure,
prepare Pure Love's golden substance,
as an alchemist mindfully
mixes and measures.

Equal amounts of four purifying parts
make the Love potion a sudden reality.
Combine the four and Love shall start.
For Love is the fifth thing coming to be,
earned by the pure in heart, reaching far
above, within and below, like the tree.

Start with one cup of seeing the true self clearly,
facing every attribute surrounding your name.
Add one cup of accepting the total self dearly,
embracing previous praise, blame, loss or gain.
Stir one cup of value, whirling assets and liabilities,
for the bowl is life's circle and experience it contains.

Break down and release old limitations,
where past wounds have become rigid formations,
like "not being good enough," a common concern,
and other self-obstacles you may discern.
Surface false beliefs, legacies of past pain,
purify hearts of history's stress and strain.

Use mortar and pestle, pressing to obtain
life's precious wisdom, the powder that remains.
We repeat experiences in search of wisdom,
a weightless substance each soul must gain.

Bless all things past, precious and profane
Throw no longer needed remnants
with conviction into the rainbow flames.
Breathe the rising smoke of Spirit
into your body's purified veins.

Now, pour upon all else the fourth and final part,
the Psyche's elixir for a catalyzing start—
Show the hidden self to the world as your art.
Multiplying the mixture in your vast heart,
the surprise cup shows the soul's sacred sparks.

Set the mixture under the Central Sun,
and experience the moment of rebirth.
Listen for your soul's vibration and song,
your own rhythms to move and sing along.
Watch for Creator's gifts at your birth,
revealing your original substance and worth.
Now you have grown Pure Love from within,
a lustrous pearl, bursting from radiant skin.

For we do not receive more love than
we love our own authentic selves,
for no matter how another loves us,
what we receive matches the inner self.

So ponder this Love equation,
and all that it wonders and may explain.
Experiment as a Learner of Love.
Find what your chalice will contain.
Persevere to create the Fifth thing—
a stone deep inside of you.

Meet one who matches the Inner Lover,
one who inevitably arrives when due.
Love comes at the appointed time.
Love shows its pure self—golden and true.

Love may grow with one or two
who are already present and in view,
or it appears with ones who come anew.

Once we fully love and accept ourselves,
perhaps we can love the world as well,
as if it is an intimate circle of a few.

Come, walk with me for a while.
Find whether this is a deep desire.
Find whether this is likely or true. ❊

I am the Prize

I am the prize, I do surmise,
drums the flicker bird, bright and wise.

Looking from within this bronze vessel,
and then back through my deep eyes:
what gifts would I proffer or sell
to be Loved as the Lover of I?

While upon this rock I stand,
watching love journeys of woman and man,
on what courage would I dare call
for love's soothing, sweet lemon balm?

Looking with blinders on my eyes
so that through matters I can see:
from the sun, an eagle spots his prey
while the fish is still beneath the sea.

The prized fish within the waters
knows its worth is dear.
The eagle flies great distance,
lightning speed and focus, clear.

I would give the world's treasure
for love where Great Spirit blows,
making birth paths and God's measure,
standards each soul deigns to know.

Looking from within this bronze vessel,
and then back through my deep eyes:
what gifts would I proffer or sell
to be Loved as the Lover of I?

I would turn around from things profane.
I'd lose useless habits and leeching fears
for Love worth the sacred and mundane
coming for me in life's golden years.

I'd venture deep space and earth's hidden core,
brave deep waters to find my shore.
I'd embrace all tender flaws,
making Love's perfection my cause.

Yet to be Loved as the Lover of I,
for God, I have already done these things.
It is now for me to answer the call
when Pure Love finally sings.

I am loving like the sunset and rain.
I am rising from tests of the bane.
Now the complex seems quite plain—

We are the prize, as we can all surmise,
drums the flicker bird, bright and wise.
We are the prize when we Love purely
and when we do as God devises.

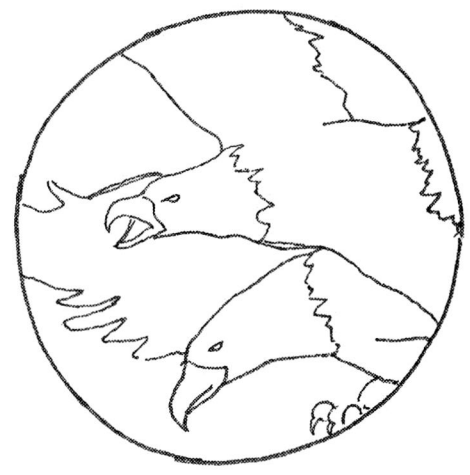

Be Love, Beloved

See Love, not seek Love.
For the seeking heart
finds its own hidden holes,
not a heart courageous and bold.

Speak Love, not ask for it.
For the asking heart
requests what it cannot give.
Gifts of truth and acceptance make Love live.

Be Love, not yearn for Love.
For the yearning heart
devours its Lover unknowingly,
making nourishment for its own needs.

Be Love and you are Beloved.
You are the Fruit and you are the Seed.
Be Love, Beloved.
Let this be your Creed. ♦

Reflections:

Chapter Four.

Love and Discernment

Desire's Illusions, Love's Reality

Love gets blamed for a lover's poor perceptions,
emotions shaping pattern recognition,
snowy static screens in the brain's reception.

Perhaps it is not Love, but desire instead,
causing us to see wanted potentials
rather than actualities we dread.

Could it be Love that strikes a person blind,
running from shadows where the Truth hides?
No, Pure Love forges a path for the Truth.
It beckons us, saying, "Seek and ye shall find."

When Pure Love flows through,
it opens the heart so that we can see
the energy of what is and images of what might be.

Pure Love enhances the wealthy human brain,
expands consciousness, opens the heart's domain,
helping us create, and unify again and again.

Love brings harmony to the body's symphony,
playing chords, calling all creatures wild and free,
singing, "Come and find joy. Revel in me."

Love's reality says, "I behold all that is you."
Together, we are different, and all the same.
Desire's illusions show images we want to view:

He gives her illusions of love she desires.
She gives him illusions of freedom he requires.
Desire's a daring rush, improvised on tight wires.

Love is caring and need not plead her case.
Just her existence enlightens and radiates.
Bask in Love's warmth. Come live at her place.

Desire's passion links us to awesome potential.
Pure Love senses and accepts what is real.
Honoring them both creates visions we can feel. ▼

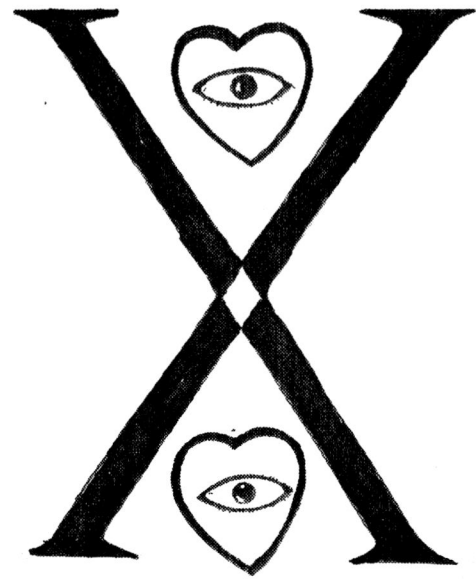

Can You See Me?

Can you see me?
Do you see through the mystery of my ways?
Do you make new space for what I do and say,
or sort my expressions into files already made?

Can you see me?
Sun can blind vision as a new day arrives.
Memories can cause illusion in love-weary eyes.
Soften your look, then learn how to gaze.

I'm in the air you breathe.
I warm the fire in your root.
You stand steady on my firm ground
You taste the variety of my fruit.

Smell the jasmine in my flower.
Sit with me in the unrushed hour.
Hear my silky smooth sounds,
coursing to places way down.

Can you see me?
Maybe yes, perhaps only later.
In your dark amber eyes, it is fear,
more than Love, I see in their mirror.

I hold the mirror, and deeply gaze
peering through desire's fiery haze.
In the mirror's reflection I begin to see
my hidden fears staring back at me.

Fear blocks the inner eye's sun,
triggering images past for the moment begun.
Whether we run or stand still,
love lingers in the air, has its own will.
We give love birth and the deed is done.
Love just is, but waits for no one.

Fear paralyzes and blinds,
or activates us to heal free.
Can you see me?
I'm only a promise of love that can be. ♒

If All Remains the Same

Stand at the precipice
of life ending, life beginning anew.
If all remains the same,
do you still choose to Jump the Broom?

For we may not know the curves ahead
or the turns each one may want to take.
We do know the path we've traveled so far.
Is this the future we want to make?

Past is not a predictor of the future absolute.
Reparation, Acts of God and Healing may undo
generations of misdeeds, coming home to roost.

Still, when we would marry another,
one critical question comes plain—
"Knowing what we know as of now,
if, between us, all remains the same
are we still happy to make this vow?"

Even when we know what we are doing,
the Universe is constantly moving.
We don't control results we're pursuing,
yet the present shows the future we're choosing,
looking beneath the rocks we're perusing—
if—all—remains—the—same. ✠

Dance of Commitment and Change

Change always comes for at least one in a pair,
yet free will is yours to act, accept or be in despair.
Commitment is not a death sentence with a chance of pardon.
It's a choice to dance together through diverse terrains and gardens.

Sometimes, it's a tango, with sultry drama and flair.
Sometimes, it's a salsa, passion and fire filling the air.
Sometimes, one watches, the other privately entertains.
Sometimes, you dance free on separate mountain ranges.
Sometimes there's a test with a winner and a loser,
easily forgetting that you both began as "choosers."

No need to manufacture change and its possibilities.
Evolution points the way. Choose the path to go or stay.
Our fears and hopes tell us where we need to grow—
Find your breakthrough zone within the self,
and a new relationship, you'll come to know.

In this light, at least one question comes to fore:
If you never changed yourself would life be a bore?
If the answer is "yes," contemplate and pursue this drill—
Would your lover feel betrayed if you change,
or love the newfound you still?

After all, with the "past you" the lover promised forever to stay.
The "future you" is a surprise, now coming the lover's way.
Isn't it a miracle how life's changes can always birth
opportunities handled well, increasing a couple's worth?

And that's the dance of commitment and change:
to stay engaged, while nothing stays the same.
When the crisis comes, to "the third thing" we can go:
commitment to the relationship beyond ego.

Whether you stay or go, handle love's crises
with all the love you know. ✡

Circle the Triangle

It takes at least one, two, three to see
the whole of a two-party relationship—
its past, present and what it can be.
The third can be a witness or friend,
a counselor, trespassing interloper,
or one who arrives soon after the end.

Circle the triangle and you will soon see
messages your Soul intended to send
from the beginning until the very end.
Place the parts in the whole's clarity.
A three-way mirror helps find verity.

"One" is a man who lost his wife.
Full of anger and pain was he,
so shocked by this new reality:
"How could she take away our life?"
Many moments built the choice to walk—
walls of silence barring intimate talk,
broken promises, rage and disrespect,
control, fights, threats and wars of sex.

"One's" heart shut down to protect itself,
seeking Denial's strength and Spirit's wealth.
Business was safe, images of intimacy hurt,
but only he could live in this barren desert.

"Two" made it the hard cold type of break,
her acts precluding any return to make.
She burned bridges, declared war, cried "Victim."
She ordered restraints for anger's symptoms.

"Three" touched "One's" wounds of armored pain.
She sang soothing sounds over love's remains.
"Three" sensed ancient anger, despondent guilt,
and saw visions of Love's School, wanting to be built.

"Two" built a legal fortress to keep "One" out.
"One" protested, resigned, and then tossed about.
Remorseful, he relinquished any legal clout.
He chose old companions—Resentment and Doubt.
"One" and "Two's" actions used all their clout
to say "I'm committed here, but I really want out!"

"Three" was a light, shining full of hope,
coming to share healing and other perspectives,
pointing to rubies amidst romantic wreckage.
As a friend, she decided to bring love's message.

"Three" knew there wasn't much "One" could give.
His work now was to heal and merely to live.
"Three" enjoyed each moment's awakening gifts.
She surrendered, let go, allowed love to lift.

It takes at least one, two, three to see
the whole of a two-party entity—
its past, present and what it can be.
The third can be a witness or a friend,
a counselor, a trespassing interloper,
or one who arrives soon after the end.

I was one arriving after the end.
I could see the circle coming
'round the triangle once again. ●▲

Mr. Man

The Beast, the Man, the Spirit—
there are three of you.
For whom does my love light?
Who comes into view?

Mr. Beast consumes me ravenously,
yet hungers always for more.
He attacks without warning suddenly,
knocking down all of my doors.

Love is a hunt for him and his guide,
both enjoying a victory won.
Standing above his prey with pride,
he stores the spoils once the deed is done.

Don't get me wrong, 'cause I love all three.
Mr. Man can't get himself together
to be together and be here with me.

Mr. Man provides for the woman he loves,
presuming she follows the basic plan—
No matter the deeds he does,
by his side is where she must stand.
He protects her from others, not from him,
believing this is what it means to love.

Mr. Man is truly the hidden one,
convinced that love he cannot survive.
Love surfaces shadows under the sun,
while he plays games and seeks to hide.

Don't get me wrong, 'cause I love all three.
Mr. Man can't get himself together
to be together and be here with me.

Mr. Spirit loves me deeply and freely—
coming in visions and dreams, he abides.
Great Spirit has his accountability,
as he pours out his heart, no games, no lies.
Mr. Spirit keeps deals in the light of day
not letting Mr. Man's ego get in the way.
Spiritual agreements are more important than
the swings of psychological woman or man.

Mr. Spirit may get all three together
in the wholeness he has the power to lead.
But if Mr. Man doesn't get himself together,
that's still no reason for me to flee,
as long as I get myself together
to be together and be here for me.

So I fall in love with the Animal,
the Woman, and the Spirit in me.

Ms. Woman moves on to heal herself
with the Wholeness living within all three.
All my parts fall in Love with the Power and Grace
of the Woman I was born to be. ෴

I Knew the Ice Would Come to Me

It was only a handshake refused,
and other orchestrations he used
to demonstrate removing a person from his life.

I shivered in the ice cold blast of wind,
blowing through on a hot summer's day.
Ice came with each refusal I saw,
while I stood near its path, waiting for its thaw.

What love and pain are buried beneath
grave decisions to discard one's friend?
Double-edged betrayal breaks from its sheath,
slashing love and trust to their end, while
signaling a permanent ice age to begin.

I froze, speaking volumes with my silence,
pondering meanings of what I had seen.
Samurai swords would've been warmer.
Dynamite would've caused me less alarm,
as I realized the ice would some day come to me.

I don't challenge the choice he made to end
close relations with a trusted student or friend.
I don't pretend to know the betrayals or codes broken
by deeds done or private words publicly spoken.
But I knew as clearly as I knew my first kin,
that some day, this ice would come to me.

Whatever we do to one friend,
we may do to another in the end.
The same perceived circumstances
trigger the chain of events again.

Yes, people can and do change.
Things fall apart and we can begin again,
beyond our old limits, and into new terrain.

This is free will and choice,
and the need for change has a distinct voice.
So I looked around and listened closely,
for the sounds of a shift coming soon.
Hearing silence, I knew the ice would come to me.

Fire and ice intensely mix to make stone.
Mountains are born, living when we are gone.
Yes, we laughed and frolicked in our fire.
We danced and made prayers that still inspire.
Still, I knew the ice would come to me.

I knew not the moment, the minute or the hour
love would lose deep color and fragrant flower.
or what great or minute thing would bring
cause for your danger alarms to ring.
Yet, I knew the ice would come to me. △

I've Been to the Movie, I've Seen the Picture Show

I've been to the movie,
I've seen the picture show.
It's time to start acting like
I know which way things will go.

It would be different if I'd never seen
this gripping plot unfold before.
Then I could respond with amazement
as the tale twists and turns at my door.

We pursue and create the dramas
we've already watched at length,
while claiming we know the end
and truths this epic story can send.

Then we tell a recent version as if it's new,
with results we are surprised to find.
We say "I couldn't believe it!", although
we've told the same story many times.

If you enjoy the movie, keep seeing it again.
Recharge your batteries with its energy.
Use it to escape, educate or to entertain.
You're co-directing these shenanigans.

Or make a new movie, write a new story line.
Break through old patterns with a creative mind.
Heal the self, if new results you seek to find,
'cause in love we're all being paid in kind.

We take our lives to a higher level,
a unique vibe each of us can reach,
whenever we learn the lessons
our dramas confess and seek to teach.

Then we can say this truth:

"I've been to the movies,
but I haven't lived this picture show.
I'm living a new adventure,
claiming new paths to grow." ♦

That's Not Spirit Telling You to Forget About Love

It may be exhaustion and doubt,
even fear of being tossed about,
but that's not Spirit telling you
to forget about love.

It may be stubbornness and pain,
some demon making you insane.
But that's not Spirit telling you
to forget about love.

Don't stay secluded,
get rested and get renewed.
Only this time, know the war
to win is the battle within.
Then walk love's way again.
Give it up and surrender.
Release old patterns you defend.

Be grateful for love's iterations,
moving toward your emancipation,
'cause that's not Spirit telling you
to forget about love. ☾

A Long Walk in the Desert

I took a walk in the rain with him one day,
with no thoughts of a drought coming our way.
We walked slowly through these mossy woods.
Hands clasped, we were soaked by pouring rain,
with only our skin for jackets and only the forest for hoods.

I looked deeply into his eyes,
and listened to my Inner Voice so wise.
There, I discerned a likely reality:
"This could be a long walk in the desert,
a walk without any water for me."

Still I took the walk into joy and strife,
knowing the journey may not be for life,
but for a few years, months, weeks or days.
Why? It was the chance to discern form from its mirage,
to discern the look of love from desire's gaze.

Suddenly, one day all water turned to dust,
showing peripheral visions leading me to self-distrust.
Yes, the storm's intensity had drawn me instantly to him.
Yet the aftermath of our adventure left me hanging, out on a limb.
Swinging in thin air, I was asking myself,
"Where is the firm ground?
Why is life's light now so dim?"

I awoke at sunrise one morning,
and walked by the Mother's fertile ceremonial womb.
It was something we had built together,
now seeming like an empty barren tomb.
Although I walked on fertile land, my heart was in a deserted place.
Walking in the heart's desert, tears poured water onto my face.
I remembered promises of union, wisdom, and feasts of consciousness.
I had fed myself dream fruit that was not yet ripe.
I was in a surreal painting, after feasting on still life.

Discernment was here at the beginning, watching me,
flashing frames of actual and potential truths I could see.
I ran with my feelings, hoping for what might be.
I ran with no fear of crashing, which was a possible reality.
I was invested in love's romance as my preferred reality.

I went from a walk in mossy woods
to a desert that was foreign to me.
I came through this desert-love initiation,
and then ate a ripe peach from my own Tree.
I was powered and fed by Love deep inside of me.

Yes, this journey was a long walk in the desert,
a long walk without any water for me.
I learned to bathe in the sand, to drink the desert's dry air.
I danced in Great Spirit's Hands, a heart transcending despair.
On a long walk in the desert without any water for me,
I learned to swim in the mercy of my own heart's sea.

I sowed an even Greater Love than I had sought to reap.

What's More Important, Control or Love?

What is more important, Control or Love?
What can feed the many, making little into plenty,
not with illusions or tricks, but with Love's substance
as the mix—light, birthed into nurturing form?

You refuse a plate of Love served warm,
a feast for the long fasting heart.
You seek instead Control's diverse buffet,
promising safety to those who take part.

Control has false safety for the young and old,
seasoning its dishes with death's choke hold.
Control blocks Love's path into a silver chalice,
while it promises illusions of a golden bowl.

For those seeking safety from abandonment,
obsession with Control serves no cure.
For Control serves a buffet that starves the heart.
Life is a narrow world of joys endured.

Control's diverse dishes each taste the same.
The more you eat, the more you need.
Control's devotees seek the one dish that feeds.
The hungry are lured, yet hunger doesn't fade.

Love's plate surprises with distinct tastes.
The more they share, the more is there.
Love's devotees are nourished and do not waste.
The hungry are lured, and hunger is cured.

Control will import clean water,
while it poisons the local natural source,
pretending to make life better for the people
while destroying the healing life force.

I'd take a plate of grass or a bowl of wood
to build a life of Love and Works understood.
Pass me a plate of Love served warm to start.
I'll share mine with the fast-breaking hearts.

What is more important, Control or Love?
What can feed the many, making little into plenty,
not with illusions or tricks but with Love's substance
as the mix—light birthed into nurturing form.

We're all born with a taste for Love's feast
that Control's buffet can never appease.
Discover how Love's feast can sustain us all,
manifesting a bountiful harvest for Fall.

End the fast of the unloving heart.
Fast from Fear, Greed and Hatred instead.
It is for the sake of one of these three
that Control's buffet has always been fed. ❄

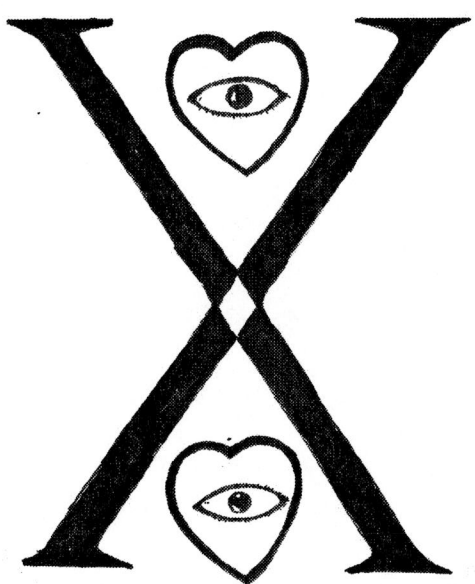

A Gift is a Gift

A gift is a gift and a trade is a trade.
A purchase is something for which money is paid.
Loans can feel like gifts, but are debts to be paid—
Four ways to share energy in this world we've made.

Some come bearing gifts, while wanting a trade,
one hand offering, the other waiting to be paid.
Some rejoice for gifts they later find are loans,
gifts the giver retrieves when the ties are gone.

Some keep accounts of gifts given and received,
awaiting a gift of thanks before feeling pleased.
Others tire rapidly of gift-giving competitions,
and give generously based on private premonitions.

I love a gift that's a gift, a trade that's a trade,
and a purchase free and clear with money I've paid.
I love showering gifts upon blankets laid,
marking new beginnings for which I've prayed.

I tire of gifts that aren't gifts, residues from trades,
loans for stolen lands with karmic debts gone unpaid.
Love flows freely between systems who share unafraid,
discerning motives of offers accepted and made.

Let's give gifts and let's make trades.
Let's purchase and lend when we can
afford to risk not being repaid, because—
A gift is a gift, and a trade is a trade. ✡

What We're Offering, What We Want

Everybody wants Pure Love,
from Earth, All Around, Within and from Above.
Who is offering Pure Love,
to Earth, All Around, Within and to Above?
Love Economics running through all domains,
a current of life force joining all planes.

Start developing your supply
because demand's going higher and higher.
People stand in line, hoping to receive
something all of us could offer and need.

Pure Love seeks to meet each other's needs—
What do I want and what are you offering?
What am I offering and what do you want?
Let's clear Love's Fields of residue, please.

Peace and Harmony require all having what we need,
all parties self-empowered, and following their own leads.

If we want to form alliances of any kind,
Love's supply and demand are key to the design.

If we look at history, we have to face some facts.
Some steal what's not offered, then try to sell it back.
They wanted the gold, so they plundered and stole,
taking the land and riches from the First People's hold.

They wanted the oil, so they claimed the war's spoils.
Warriors die for profits, not rights of people who toil.
They wanted the land, so they twisted Christ's Plan,
invading and terrorizing First Peoples' clans.

It's time to go forward with new ways to live and heal.
First, we speak some truths and settle some old deals.
I love this Country and it's time to face some facts.
We've built prosperity with dishonorable acts.

I love this Country with a Love soft and tough,
no time to hide shadows with party-line fluff.
I love a Warrior and grieve all lives that are lost.
What can I surrender not to pay this cost?

For all Nations to work together as a Whole,
first tell our truths, and settle debts that are old.
We offer Love to all Nations who show up,
learning how Love Economics fills our cups.

For all to pull together, we have to line up within—
Speak truth, forgive, repair and then begin again.

If this doesn't make sense and we need help to take it in—

"A lot of confessin' comes before forgivin' begins, so
take forks from our tongues, look from start to end, and
take yo' hands out' my pocket and yo' knives out' my back
if ya really wanna gimme some skin." ☒

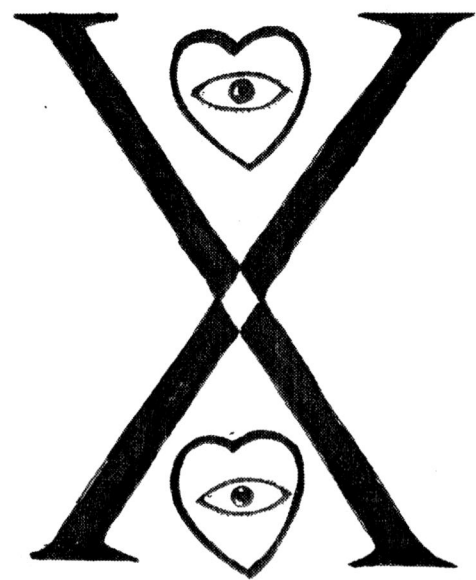

Love's Trust

I trust you to be who you are.
I trust me to see who you are,
but only when I discern reality
through the eyes of my God,
not the needs of personality.

So you always ask me what I am doing with you,
as if I'm not seeing who you are and what is true.
When it comes to loving you, I see the possible,
potential, probable and actual realities for you and me.

They come like flashes of light,
no promise to stay in plain sight
and make light into matter we count on and see.

I've had my wants and my wishes for the way things will turn out.
When emotions take over, discernment sometimes gets tossed out.

Today the potential inspires me, the actual magnetizes me,
the possible frightens me and the probable enlightens me.
Tomorrow, the actual may preclude me, while the probable depresses me,
the potential eludes me, and the possible deludes me.

This roller coaster of emotions
made me remember something Spirit taught through my devotion—

"It is best not to discern realities with emotions
or even with desires, for these waters and fires
are fed by the psyche, and not Divinely inspired.

So end the reign of the Psychological Wound
and live as one whose heart is attuned.
Release the Genius who lives within.

Discern each day's realities,
from dawn to evening and evening to dawn.
Empower and trust the Spirit within
to show pathways choices have drawn."

So I followed the Guidance
stepping up to the focus I require,
to enhance the promised gift again.
For discernment is a gift inherent within,
for Disciples of the Self who aspire.

I threw my all into the Divine Fire,
a Circle of Fire tempering personal will.
I chose to see clearly what was mine to be seen,
risking appearing alone, and moving worlds, while still.

For one who resolves the psyche
through Initiations in God's Love,
dies and is born again.

Coming back through the fire,
Initiates have a known trust of wealth
in covenants with the Higher, not the lower, Self.

I came through that fire on the shortest day and longest night,
meeting a Salamander in the cold at dawn.
I spoke these words to myself,
out loud on new winter's breath
to make sure I gained from the ashes what was left:

"I trust you to be who you are.
I trust God to see who you are.
I trust me to discern what is revealed, and
to heed instructions shown beneath the Seal.
Of all these trusts, it is a priority to learn
trust in my discernment, trust in God's will.
Trust is a gift given that still must be earned."

When I earn this gift, I have the right to say
to any person or group, near or far away:

"I trust you to be who you are.
I trust me to see who you are.
Only then will I know whether to start
trusting you to care for my heart." 〰

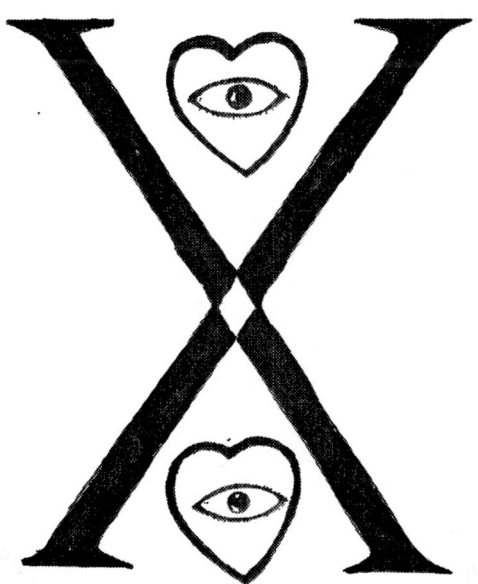

Reflections:

Chapter Five.

When it's Time to Go

We Were

We were secret lovers,
not to others but to ourselves,
who thought we hid the obvious
from eyes and ears
that could tell.

We were close,
such that our mouths were as one,
no mouths were between us,
all was said and done.

Now there are mouths—
mouths with snatches of dejection,
hurt pride and confusion,
swelling eyes and lips,
and intermittent hours of
superficially plated conversation—
which if replayed would
have no evidence of thought,
passion or contact,
no sign of knowing or being
two who were once joined at the hips
and who were one with their lips.

We were such that
I wondered why we hadn't been
good enough to ourselves,
giving one another
to ourselves.

Every choice to withhold
made our love old,
scaling its death, taking its breath—
until it was time to go.

We—were—not—true.
What—do—lovers—do?
We—were—not—true.
Nothing—else—to—do.
We were not true. ❉

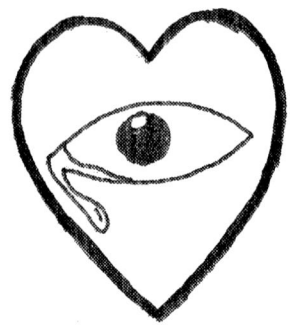

Psychic Wail

I remember when 3 o'clock in the mornin'
represented good times, down home
funky rhyme times.

With music of mind or melody,
smoke and warm, close bodies
and—oh lawdie—sweet child,
it was natural and good
to feel, and to say:

"It must be 3 o'clock in the mornin' y'all."

How soon we forget....

Now when I think of 3 o'clock in the mornin',
I really see 3 o'clock as if the clock's
hands are locked in place,
moving through the air, then
through my mind,
frozen and entombed.

And through the house with the pieces
of our breaking family grieving
in three different rooms,
I can feel the connected
disconnectedness
frozen. In space.

We are locked into place
by lasers with the strength
of steel, lasers of choices
leaving us with ruins
you don't want to
rebuild, after vows
we both killed.

Silent moans and screeches keep me awake,
and the quiet makes an unbearable noise
throughout the long night's
non-sleep. ⌂

If It Hasn't Happened

If it hasn't happened in three seconds,
three minutes, three hours, three days—
if it hasn't happened in three weeks,
three months, three seasons, or three years—
if it hasn't happened by now, we've probably seen
whatever will be happening for me and you.

Commitment's not happening for me and you.
That's the way it's been, and it's still true.
Yes, it's possible and potential above and below,
but it's not alive or real on the earth we know.

It hasn't happened in three seconds,
three minutes, three hours, three days,
not in three months, three seasons,
not in three years has it come into play.
Can't think of a reason to hang around to see
if we'll break the trend we've set to be.

It was a dream, all in my head, held by a line
on the end of some player's gaming reel.
Each time he caught me, he threw me back in,
and I swam free until I ate the bait again.
Without the dream, there's no lure to catch.
"Dream the dream again, and get a better match."

I'm the first to say "anything is possible."
Caterpillars do become butterflies,
and in some dimensions, Elephants do fly.

Caterpillars climb up from the ground,
and take a long, dreaming rest.
They are dreaming potentials that will soon be found
flying their colors past the Robin's nest.

Humans can go through seasons, year after year,
no metamorphoses conscious in our tiny spheres.
For many, there's no noticeable change
in the past minutes, hours, days,
months, seasons, or years.

The Caterpillar has a dream and a focus,
an intent, design and will--all directed to the beauty
the Butterfly's metamorphosis reveals.
We have not spoken our shared dream,
nor rested jointly in the dormant cocoon.

Perhaps this tells us to dream our own dreams
of who we are and who we are born to be.
I am moving in my own metamorphosis,
painting my face and my wings in the dream.
I am preparing to fly to a place prophesied,
where we envision Love's reality in the Winter
and we transfigure our past in the Spring. ∎

Takin' Myself Out' the Game

Takin' myself out' the game
'cause time's not right for me.
Maybe some day'll be my time.
Today, love's not workin' for me.

Gonna take some time,
doing some things for me—
dreams I've had all my life
can now come true to be.

A woman can have trouble
putting her mind on other dates
when she's got her life on hold
for the love of her chosen mate.

I came into this life
with a lot of love to give.
Helping people every day
is how I choose to live.

So, I'm takin' myself out' the game
'cause time's not right for me.
Maybe some day'll be my time.
Today, love's not workin' for me.

Gonna take some time
doing some things for me—
Dreams I've had all my life
can now come true to be.

Love is a funny thing.
It's a certain kind of wealth.
No matter how much you're taking in,
giving Love is good for your health.

Maybe I'll go for the Big Love,
and throw myself into Spirit's Hands.
Turn myself over to Her and find
what manner of love She has in mind. ⌘

How We Open and Close

When one person appears to move slow,
and the other imagines moving fast,
and they both want their connection to last,
see if Spirit's words to me are timely seeds to sow:

"It will unfold when he wants it to unfold.
It'll be over when you say it is over,
and that's how you will open and close.
That way, this love will never be old.
It takes two to open love's doors.
It takes two to close love out.
Meanwhile, seize lessons of what
your connection is all about."

So one day I gently said this to him,
with my own words for what Spirit said was true:

"It will unfold when you want it to unfold.
It will be over when I say it's over,
and sometimes it is already over
before it begins, my Dear Friend.

This play is not because either one of us
is more powerful or has total control,
but because we agreed long ago as souls—
"These energies for one another, we will hold:"

You, to send lightning as we meet,
me to fall swiftly off my seat.
Me, to make a space for you to be,
you, to catalyze my creativity.
You, to open doors to your ways,
me, to nurse wounds others made.
You, to thrill me with honor and charm,
me, to ignore the heart's warning alarms.

You, to play games of hide and seek,
me, to vocalize what others fear to speak.
You, to maintain the element of surprise,
me, to ground you through the gaze of my eyes.
You to pursue me impulsively, but from within a fence,
making moves followed with ambivalence.
Me to respond slowly and excitedly,
then get fatigued with your resistance.

You, to play games to pull me in,
but when I call the hand, you fold to win.
Your hand? Be angry, frightened and resist.
My hand? Be Love's eternal presence that persists.
Next round? You, to hesitate and be late.
Me, to walk away and to wait.

Meanwhile, I move on with my life.
You wonder whether love outlasts strife.
Both of us restock the inner powers of our stores.
We stay at a distance, keeping slightly open doors.

These roles and hands we can change any time,
since the truth seems underneath, quite sublime.
Still, we each agreed to hold the polar end
of all hopes and fears the other brings in.

Then suddenly I realize, this is real life for us two,
not a rehearsal, but a premier showing and review.
We each have our roles and familiar reactions.
There's really no need for a new call for "Action!"
No need to wonder if our potential will unfold.
No need for lights to flash and for cameras to roll.

Now I see that the nature of our Play is this—
It is over whenever, however, and before it begins.
We have loved before and come now to shed old skins.
We have already done the Beginning.
We have already done the Middle.
We have already done the End.
This is what it has been already.
This is what it will still be, ever steady.

For us, no more whining, boos or thrilling applause.
For us, no more icy stages followed by warming thaws.
No more wondering when, if or how.
No more willing—just filling the stillness,
after the rippling awakening sound
of the drummers' last beat has been pounded,
speaking the truth the world around—
That-this-is-not-an-interim-round!

Yes, I know what I said before—
"It will unfold when you want it to unfold.
It will be over when I say it's over."
And that's how we always open and close.
No matter how it appears, in the End—
I know we do it together, dear Friend. ♦

Dear God, Can I Die Now?

Would you rather die than make a true, deep change,
leaving others you can't seem to deeply rearrange?
Has your identity become tied to and confused
with habits, people and things you don't want to lose?
On life's stage do you want to take a final bow?
Are you asking, "Dear God, can I die now?"

"I can't face starting over again," says she.
"It's too late in life for me to be free.
But he's not changing and that's clear to me.
I swore I would never get a divorce.
There must be a way out with no remorse.
Dear God, can I die now?"

"Love has never worked out for me," says he.
"I'm living alone with no responsibility,
attached to old patterns that block intimacy.
Unless I'm really willing to change myself,
starting up again is bad for everyone's health.
Dear God, can I die now?"

"I've changed myself and helped others too," says she,
"sharing wisdom that you gave to me, with people preferring familiarity.
I'm exhausted and grateful for the life I've lived,
achieving more than I thought life would give.
Dear God, can I die now?"

"Between us, I was supposed to die first," says he.
"Now she's taken her virtues and left me to grieve,
a guilty, caring parent, with no freedom to leave.
I hardly meet my own needs, like hunger and thirst,
while facing those who think I should've died first.
Dear God, can I die now?"

God spoke back to them all:

"You can survive this way, but not thrive,
feeling that it's a chore for you to be alive.
Dying without changing is still form rearranging,
without resolving and evolving into the potential
that is you! Bring DEATH to the limits blocking you.

"Find the Healer and meet the Teacher,
Take the Medicine, watch the Creatures.
Hear the Knower, track the Way Shower,
fire the Controller, hire the Spirit Holder.
Release the old pattern and kill the limit.
Right life's wrongs and get on with living it!

"Then ask the question and perhaps get a blessing:
'Can I die now?' And, I'll answer you too.
From where I sit in the Universal view,
whenever you die, you're still not through.
For Death is Life lived in another room."

So finish the journey in the body,
and do first what you have tried to flee.
You'll find the Love of Life there,
and then come on time to room with Me. ⌘

I Wish You Well

I wish you well,
as I can't hold you
beyond your mercurial will.

I wish you well,
as hope dies in me,
while love's enigma lives still.

Four simple words
must be enough to tell
what my heart knows so well.
My darling love,
I wish you well.

You're not offering what I want.
I must not be what you need.
Nothing's left for me to give
to one busy trying not to live.

It's not 'cause I'm so understanding.
It's not 'cause I happen to agree.
It's not 'cause life's too demanding
with our love's intensity.

It's 'cause my life's renewing
while you can't wait to go on.
I can't live for you and me
and bring dreams from dark to dawn.

Right now with all these feelings,
I have no other words to tell.
I can only say my dearest,
"I wish you well.
I wish you well.
I wish you well." ♥

Maybe it's Time to Let Go

If you are the only person
choosing to be in the pair—
If you're the only one bringing
gifts of love and steady care—
Maybe it's time to let go.

If you express love stripped and bare,
and your partner's heart never opens—
If love's actions and vulnerable words
are never truly done and spoken—
Maybe it's time to let go.

If love is a war zone
where you are murdered
and left to die alone—
If neither are willing to remove
the seeds of destruction sown—
Maybe it's time to let go.

If you would rather destroy the Innocents,
than protect and feed those in your care—
If fear and appearances seem more important
than transforming and being self-aware—
Maybe it's time to let go.

If you think you've got all the lessons
and are willing to share the blessings—
If despite third party assistance,
you're not willing to go the distance—
Maybe it's time to let go.

If you love another completely,
and the person doesn't love you back,
there's no reason to kill your love—
just gather yourself and pack.
Maybe it's time to let go.

But no one made you to hold on.
No one can force you to let go.
Each one must walk out love's visions.
Each one must know when to let go.

◇◇

Reflections:

Eight Poems for Endings

1. Love Lives On
Turn at the sun. Go to the moon.
Love's form goes soon.
Love lives on through June. ❖

2. Dogs are Loyal
Dogs are loyal.
You're a coyote "wannabe" dog,
who wants to become royal. ☾

3. The Punisher's Gift
The Punisher's gift becomes a lift
after the dreaded rift
is done. ♦

4. The Violated Me
The Violated me is now the Heroic me
come to Love thee.
Thanks. ♓

5. Celebrate Our Ending
Celebrate our ending as we began.
Life and death do flow together
at the river's bend. ♒

6. "So-and-So is 'Daid'"
When the relationship is over,
be sure it is said:
"So-and-so is 'daid'. Good." ♥

7. Make New Space
Something dead is taking up space.
Clean the insides.
The dead have a new place. ♑

8. Bless the Dead
Bless and speak well of the dead,
for they have more access to your head.
Good. ✡

Reflections:

Chapter Six.

Calling Love Warriors

Love is a Sacred Space

Love is not a deed or a license.
It's a location, a sacred place.
Love shifts the shape of any room,
enticing lovers to create.

If you want to live in Love with me,
stay a while, fill this space.
We co-create purposeful life,
birthing worlds that regenerate.

Love doesn't give us permission
to control what one another does.
If that's the price we have to pay,
we'd be imprisoned with Love as the cause.

I love you from the untouched depths,
virgin waters of a deep, dark sea.
I love you from my body's bones,
the stones that store blood's history.

If you want to live in Love with me,
let's create the sacred space,
meeting one another's needs
as best we can in this place.

Still, our love is not a license.
It's a location, a sacred space.
It is a commitment to a "third thing,"
beyond our separateness.

With this Vision of Love,
I encircle and breathe a sacred space.
I feed the fire and listen at the door.
A Love Warrior joins me in this place.

Love's sound, touch, scent and taste
come to my hidden door.
I seek the contours of your face,
for time is here and I must have a view.
I reach through the door,
my hand on your heart, asking—
"Dear One, is that you?"

Rest the Weary Warrior and Warrioress

Rest, you weary men and women,
answering Spirit's call to Love.
Wherever we go, the work's within,
and perhaps peace lies there as well.

Bring vision, courage, and faithful works done.
Love first-in, and last-out, until the inner war is won.
Rest and retreat, weary ones, and then take heed—
There's no quick exit 'til you've done the Love deed.

Love may not appear to match images in the brain.
You must discern entry into love's diverse terrain:
seeing mossy rocks, sunflower fields, forested lush ferns,
dancing November's close embraces in new public places,
smelling lavender's scent and a summer night's ocean wind,
hearing heartfelt concerns near a winter fire's steady burn.

If you're among Love's wounded, get up and ride again.
Generate power through light, moving through your disdain.
Warriors heal their wounded hearts 'til fear is overcome.
Love the self through Spirit, and then love another free.
Heal for yourself and generations, but don't do it for me.
Brave-up in Love's sun! Heal by Love's cool moon.
Fearless Love Warriors will emerge, and not too soon. ♥

Twins Over Time

He walked into my sacred circle today,
and joined my earthly family.
He entered an ethereal gateway,
where ancestors of the body
and lineage of the soul
intersect earth's core
between two bowls.

That's how I met the energy of this man.
That's how fast we merged our diverse clans.
That's how I recognized signs of Spirit's Hand,
joining otherwise directed people,
whose personalities have different plans.

I found my other self in him, different but the same.
He mirrored the sacred and worldly in me,
and he mirrored the wild and the tame.

Periodically, we go our separate ways, and
follow different rhythms our sacred pipes play.
Still, I feel this man deep in my bones,
alive in the porous places, a spirit at home.
When I disconnected, much to my surprise
it was myself I felt, a twin the same as I.

Release fantasies of forms this energy may take.
Twin flames may or may not an earthly couple make.
Dancing intertwined or dancing apart,
twin flames forever support the other's sacred spark.
Cherish the fragile sparks or blow these out in vain.
An eternal connection exists for twin flames.

Twins over time, accept life's refrain.
Do the work and share the Love you have together—
This time on earth's plane. ✡

Sacred Woman, Sacred Man, Sacred Love

The love some carry is not designed
for only one beloved woman or man.
Some carry love born to assist us all—
love born from answering Spirit's call.

Answer the call, sacred woman and sacred man.
Form unions unfolding Spirit's divine plan.
Woven into the chosen life you both live
are secrets the Spirit reveals for you to give.

Rare are those willing to love and learn,
helping others gain wisdom to discern:
love from lust and ignorance from trust,
immortality of a woman's ashes,
the visiting legacy of a man's dust.

Few may know what matter you forsake,
living visions hearts know are true, not fake.
Few may know the blessings you faithfully receive,
turning to the Spirit for matters of need.

With timelessness of service in the material void,
God's Infinite Presence, you have fully enjoyed.
Untangling the world's hungry strings of greed,
you are holy flowers grown from Creator's seed.

Ordinary men and women living in disguise
share extraordinary stories of love's many tests,
for your love is forever strengthened and blessed
by the light that shines from Great Spirit's eyes.

The love we all carry is not designed
for only one beloved woman or man.
We each carry love born to assist us all—
love born from answering Spirit's call.

Answer the call, sacred women and sacred men.
Form unions unfolding Spirit's Divine plan.
Woven into the chosen life we all live
are secrets the Spirit reveals for us to give.

"He's" a Love Warrior

Masculine and Feminine Principles are Energy,
moving through the forms of every woman and man.
Energy rearranges to meet the needs of the Whole
until all tribes relate across all lands.
For Energy and form are not the same, allowing new forms to unfold.

A bodacious wild boar encircles her, knowing he belongs to this clan,
a clan of fire reflecting Spirit's immortality, embodied in sacred woman and man.
Dedicated to serve designs of Great Mystery, he knows of building nations with integrity.
He's a Love Warrior.

He stands easily in and near the fire's wild flames,
heating dormant restless rocks, staking his claim.
He moves like air across molten, hot waves.
With a panther's prowess he shifts shapes,
carrying Spirit's provider gene for his mate.
In love's explosions, he shares his full plate.
He's a Love Warrior.

Dragonfly dreams bring them together at the shore.
He's a responsible adventurer, of ancient lore.
He knows how to use self as a generator,
and not as a siphoning straw.
He holds the line while she births form, a pair
using masculine and feminine laws.
He's a Love Warrior.

He learns and teaches as a man for all seasons,
thinking generations in all that he reasons.
He honors her in the presence of all the clan,
for he gives himself to this woman as her man.
His commitment and word are as good as gold,
as he uses his wisdom, a universe to unfold.
He's the Hunter, he's the Healer, he's the Warrior, he's the Lover,
He's the Potential, he's the Limit, he's the Rock, he's the Water.
He's a Love Warrior.

He gives kisses upon her ear while she sleeps,
proud that she rarely has reasons to weep.
He inspires the clan in a Spirit-binding hold,
capturing wealth of their roots, buried deep.
He protects all, bringing apocalyptic relief.
He's a Love Warrior.

"She's" a Love Warrior

Masculine and Feminine Principles are Energy,
moving through the forms of every woman and man.
Energy rearranges to meet the needs of the Whole
until all tribes relate across all lands.
For Energy and form are not the same, allowing new forms to unfold.

Nothing holds her back, for her Love is in every act.
She's the root traveling to earth's core, feeding the tree needing more.
People die and people live, based on the love she can give.
She's a Love Warrior.

A lioness hunting for the pride, or the wolf's
alpha female seeking her mate far and wide,
she dies many times for love's sake, and
Love's cures are what she makes.
She has courage beyond her despair,
fighting for the esteem of those in her care.
She's a Love Warrior.

She whispers the right soothing words,
bringing stillness to a stampeding herd.
As she walks the earth, visions come into form,
and she's a mysterious weapon, even unarmed.
She carries the culture in her dark womb, and
brings faith to those wrestling with doom.
She's a Love Warrior.

She stands by her mate and by her clan,
providing hope through her virtue for her man.
She feeds the people, seeing what they need;
and she sacrifices her body as she bleeds.
If she walks away from home's door,
she's already given her all and more,
'cause she's a Love Warrior.

Through her deeds, gold standards are set.
Inspired by her actions, people do their best.
She's a Seer and a Knower, she's a Watcher and Way Shower.
She's the Goddess, she's the Temptress, she's the Strength and the Weakness.
She's the Priestess, she's the Warrioress, she's the Half and the Wholeness.
She unifies the people through her heart,
weaving the flow that is Love's art.
She's a Love Warrior. ♥

Bridging Waves and Worlds

Waves of emotion sometimes carry me,
washed ashore to moments of brilliant clarity,
then leaving me to climb mountains of mystery.

Dawn promises a pathway, with signs faintly marked.
Descending, I stumble through the familiar dark,
bumping into shadows, deeply grieving history's scars.

Lands stolen, lives taken, people stolen, lineage broken:
Burn diseased blankets and dismantle murderous ships!
Let only truth fall from our mumbling diverse lips!

Volcanic anger covers the fruits of greed seeds, molten.
Our pure roots emerge again, bringing gifts lost or stolen.
Make a bridge between us all, letting Spirit be spoken.

I see waves of light bringing hope apparently near.
Thundering hooves of warriors promising help I hear.
After the sun, blinding fog rolls in from the rear.

Thank God for loving friends and family,
reaching across desert tests and ocean mercies,
sharing stories born to wash away all our worries.
If not for loving souls, who see and touch my heart,
I would stand alone with Spirit, imagining I'm apart.

Still, I fall to my knees, begging God for true relief.
I hear, "Harvest the lavender plants. Work as you weep."
At morning's rise, Raven comes loudly to let me know
drowning waters have receded and are slowing their flow.
Let me heal now to face the world's Central Sun, because
a promise I made to assist has already begun.

We build a bridge of consciousness this time around,
to cross our troubled waters collectively, and not drown.
We lay down the tree from above, and the tree from below,
a bridge the tribes of our hearts may now cross and show—
Worlds of Wounded Separation have ended—
Begin to heal. Let it be so.

Waves of Unity are reborn and human hearts must know.
The Ripple Effect of Wholeness is growing.
Surrender. Let it flow. ✺

Love is the Power

What if Love is the Power, moving everything—
the thunder of the heavens, the blooming in the Spring?
What if Love is the Power, holding all life brings—
the movement of the waters and the song the swan must sing?

Then I will love you better
than you have ever known.
I'll love you through life's seasons.
I'll be the water on your stone.

Because Love is the Power.
Love can change the day.
Fear tastes its poisoned flower,
hatred drowns its angry flames.

Count the treasures given
by seeking to control.
Find your life's been driven
by what fear has bought and sold.

So let's take Love as the Power,
no matter what else we see.
Let love fill each hour,
joining us eternally.

Flowing from heaven's gateways,
bursting from earth's deep springs,
Love heals our wounded spaces,
and the ancients weep and sing.

Because Love is God's Power, moving everything—
the thunder of the heavens, the blooming in the Spring.
Because Love is God's Power, holding all life brings—
the movement of the waters and the song the swan must sing.

Love is God's Power, moving everything
Love is God's Power....

Fight, Flight and Light

We can wage a war, based on treatment we've received.
We can launch a campaign for unmet needs we grieve.
We can look for any savagery and scarcity we perceive.
We can unleash our trained attack dogs—
Fear and Hatred, who hide behind masks unseen.

Humans know how to attack or flee from whatever it is we fear,
an instinct to Fight or take Flight whenever danger's near.
Remember that the Light we all carry is a substance that binds.
When we work to right our wrongs and danger is in sight,
infuse and evoke instead the Power of Unifying Light.

For Love is a powerful weapon, and Light is its consummate shield,
reflecting to those who meet it, the darkest shadows concealed.
Pure Love can melt resistance, and Light carries just pursuits.
Love Warriors work for the Wholeness,
growing Justice and Harmony as fruits.

Oh come on, Fearless Warrior! Ride that courageous steed!
Bring medicine of courage, burning insecurities.
Flash the brilliant Light from Creator's quickening lead.
A worthy corps of us is left standing, sowing a Loving seed,
enlightened from blind fear, purified of hatred's needs. ♐♒

The Ripple Effect

It is the Year 2015, designated the Year of Harmony.
I sit by the water, filled with Joy and Reverie.
I celebrate the Unity we've learned throughout the years.
Like a stone breaking the surface of still water,
waves of change we started all came to alter
illusions even change agents once held dear.
Perhaps the movements started with each generation
ripple until transformation comes without limitation.

Those serious about Harmony for all humanity
found the lines we once drew in society
kept us from seeing the Universe as it really is.
All things are connected, not just the two-leggeds,
who thought they were the only beings that talked.
Expanded minds began to be able to see
the Whole Universe as a moving, talking quantum sea.

Once upon a time we all co-created strife
between the Red, Black, Yellow, Brown and White.
Now there is fluid communication
within and across all the diverse nations—
People who fly the sky, crawl the ground,
root through the Earth, make different sounds.

Was there a time when people couldn't hear
the messages in the sounds of life so dear?
Those who could were thought strange in the head.
Now Discernment is normal, like being well-read.
Receiving and sending meaning across space and time,
the Dolphins always communicated across all lines.
The Wolf tells about the star dropping in
to bring energy for Earth's morning vitamin.

The Joy of Life is in the connectedness, we say.
Diverse languages are no longer a limitation.
We hear deeper than the physical ear can play.
We appreciate words spoken as incantations,
moving us through consciousness with unique sensations
of contactful, inner tactile and complete communication.

Everyone reads what you feel, think and say
as if broadcasted in the ethers we breathe anyway.

At work and in all communities,
we know what Diversity on Earth is worth—
now that we are all from different planets
and witness unique purposes shown at birth.
It's funny to think how humans once fought,
acting like it was the qualified they sought.
Then we met other beings whose only crime
was making our strengths look like nursery rhymes.

We had proclaimed a System based on Merit's Eyes
when those from Normville rushed to ostracize
diverse beings who were geniuses skill-wise,
if they failed tests called "Be and Look Like Me,"
devised for comfort and control of Normville's "powers-that-be."

The Universe knew we'd be slow to get it right,
beings came to surround us with mirrors and light.

As usual, many of us were afraid of what we didn't know.
Then we relaxed, and let our curiosity show.
We learned to teach one another our meanings—
with moves and sounds, a brilliant picture show.
Now all human beings are truly multi-lingual,
and Star Trek even stopped making its sequels.

I have to admit it was great, finally, to lay down
attachment to oppression and regression that stayed around.
It's exciting being free to engage and move apart,
knowing our connections are all woven through the Heart.
Now, if we want to start any kind of friction and sparks
we see the wholeness of the Universe first.
And right before our eyes, our thoughts crystallize
into a product we ourselves graciously receive.

It's not like before—when the two leggeds started war,
believing we were achieving by killing one another.
Now we know that everyone's included.
We affect all by what we're thinking and doing.
Now talking to computers makes perfect sense.
After all, we made up artificial intelligence.

All nations now accept what the ancients already knew—
People come in forms other than two-leggeds—
Sea people, sky people, stone people, tree people,
and even the Cosmos as we know it has its own eggs.

There are no eternal Victims, no eternal Perpetrators
All parts of the Universe are really Co-Creators.
In 2015, it may be obvious to you and me,
but there was a time when human beings could not see
that we were the ones making up this shared reality.
The day we decided to take away the lines,
we uncovered and co-created something truly sublime.

There were people, looking like pure energy—
all in motion like tiny particles in the quantum sea.
The skins of Black, Yellow, White, Red, and Brown
weren't even the tip of Diversity now to be found.
People now understood their Indigenous Roots on Earth,
and origins we have in the broader Universe.
Our relatives from the Earth and Sky bring around
ancient stories that have been passed down.

Relationships within and between genders
were no longer something to mend.
Masculine and Feminine Energy
are essential both to women and men.
Whatever your sexual orientation, gender is balanced within.

Structures that blocked the Wholeness began to fall apart,
rearranging into Systems matching the Loving Heart.
Each group who has been Oppressed creates Liberty for the Rest,
when the Structures blocking Wholeness fall apart.
For the Wholeness has always been a Primal Force,
not some "New Age" view.

Wherever you look now, you see partially a reflection of you.
Being the Self and the Whole became Life's joyous coup.

Spiritual and scientific realities
can no longer be classified as Horror or Science Fiction
now that human consciousness has gone beyond its old restrictions.

To see Unified Spirit, Science and Art of the Universe
becomes the ultimate transformation for some people on Earth.
Meanwhile others heard the message of wisdom
from the Kingdoms and Queendoms of forests, streets and skies.
Some watched a vision of Harmony materialize
from staring deeply into Grandmother's and Grandfather's eyes.

Now when the Stone speaks we all listen.
Mother Earth tells of healing from a long illusion of Separation.
Father Sky is speaking firmly and lightning abounds.
We notice it's the same shape as the roots of plants in the ground.

Now, it's hard even to remember a time when there were lines
that stood in the way, manufacturing distance and time.

Thankfully we all learned through our co-creations
that Harmony comes when we see Unity in the Design.

First the helpers of the people agreed to balance themselves.
They were working to heal others, yet they were not well
From this agreement came their own personal transformations.

They became the Presence of the Unified Field,
assisting self-empowerment within and between all Nations.

It is the Year 2015, designated the Year of Harmony.
I sit by the water, filled with Joy and Reverie.
I celebrate the Unity we've learned throughout the years.

Like a stone breaking the surface of still water,
waves of change we started all came to alter
illusions even change agents once held dear.
Perhaps the movements started with each generation
ripple until transformation comes without limitation.

Visionary leaders make a colorful tapestry
of the Ripple Effect moving infinitely—
the Moment we make the lines disappear.

We are an idea whose time has come.
Are we ready? 〰

We're All Wading in the Water—
A Living Poem

*[Singing] "Wade in the water, wade in the water, children, wade in the water..."
The killer and the killed join to become as one,
unified until the next wave has begun.
No hiding from what we as a country have done.
Wholeness is being born, and its time has come.

[Singing] "Wade in the water, wade in the water, children, wade in the water..."
The privileged and the oppressed are jointly tied.
Upon unconscious waters, conscious minds blindly ride.
They are moved by upheavals and roaring riptides,
until monsters rise from the depths inside.

*[Singing] "My God's gonna trouble the water....."
So we prayed for a change, and a change is gon' come—
Change touching us where we'd rather be left alone.

[Singing] "My God's gonna trouble the water...."
In a great nation blinded by its shadow side,
truth sounds like fiction 'til your boat capsizes.

[Singing] "My God's gonna trouble the water..."
The privileged go darkly to find the light that hides.
Every word and deed shows our roots inside.

[Singing] "My God's gonna trouble the water...."
Now those asleep are rudely awakened,
our national beliefs irreversibly shaken.

[Singing] "My God's gonna trouble the water...."
Many are dying so that we become awake, and
break through old patterns for all our sakes.

[Singing] "My God's gonna trouble the water...."
All rights stolen are now returned.
All inequities ignored are now discerned.

[Singing] "My God's gonna trouble the water..."
Life is a Laboratory where we agreed to learn.
Racism must die. Now it's Unity's turn.

---

* Excerpts from the traditional Negro Spiritual, "Wade in the Water"

[Singing] "See that Band all dressed in Black..."
Waters and winds disturb whatever lies at the base.
Purifying ourselves, we have filth and faith to face.
Centuries of blood flows in toxic swamps and streams,
making apathy impossible as we wake from our dreams.

*[Singing] "See that Band all dressed in Red..."
Leaders come forth from fringes least expected,
where wisdom has survived amidst cultural wreckage.
People across colors and nations begin to join hands,
telling their fearless truths and taking visionary stands.

[Singing] "See that Band all dressed in Yellow..."
A new day dawns and we act with bold, clear force,
empowering self and others where integrity guides choices.
Love brings on a collective fever as our healing crisis.
New growth from Vision quickly spreads and rises.

*[Singing] "See that Band all dressed in White..."
We're all wading in the water, from all directions we come.
Our ancestors are with us, finding ways to a new home.
We're all wading in the water, and none of us are immune.
Our new Visions bear fruit because our hearts are attuned.

[Singing] See that Band all dressed in Blue...
Life is a Laboratory where we all agreed to learn.
Separation has dissolved, and Conscious Wholeness has returned.
We're all wading in the water, letting go of what we've tried and done.
When we all take responsibility, Help from an Unexpected Quarter comes.

[Singing] "Wade in the water, wade in the water, children, wade in the water.
My God's gonna trouble the water." ⚹◆❖☾✡☯☽✺🕊☩✝

I Send My Blankets Over You

I send my blankets over you,
layers of energy meant to keep you
from any that would do you harm.

I send my blankets over you,
loving sweet thoughts of truth,
all you need to keep you warm.

I send my blankets over you,
Navigator of all waters who comes anew,
for Love is a shield that disarms.

I know you don't need my protection.
I am only your heart's true reflection.
I know that having my love
opens hearts like wings of a dove.

I send my blankets over you,
kindred Spirit of Shaka Zulu,
bringing love where anxieties brew.

I send my blankets over you.
Those who've loved me, I've loved you.
I'm loving you when you're not looking.
I'm feeding you when you're not cooking.
I fall asleep in the energy of your arms,
protected by your power, vision and charm.

I know you don't need my protection.
I am only your heart's true reflection.
I know that having my love
opens hearts like wings of a dove.

I send my blankets over you.
Because saying "I love you"
may cause all kinds of alarm.

I send Blankets of Love's Light
because Blankets are Love's Vibration,
and now Truth is Love's Conversation.

So I send my blankets over you,
stepping into spaces of your essence so true,
breathing sweet nectar of our souls disarmed.

I send my blankets over you,
bringing comfort while you are blue.
Making a ring of fire, I say
"Mean spirits, be warned."

I know you don't need my protection.
I am only your heart's true reflection.
I know that having my love
opens hearts like wings of a dove,

That's why I send my blankets over you,
so your heart will never again be broken,
once you have the courage to let it open.

I send my blankets over you.
The "Marys" and Jesus send a Comforter too.
Tattooed faces bring visionary clues.
Welcoming songs call Truth into view.
Men and women of the Waitaha true,
being Warriors for Peace and for Love,
opening hearts like wings of a dove.

For Brave Warriors and Warrioresses of Lakota Sioux,
for Mayan and Incan ancestors who are coming through,
for all Spirits of the West Gate who stand in clear view,
for Choctaw, Cheyenne and Apache who are dancing too.
Ancestors of the Dogon in Mali join us too.
Nubian Blanket Carriers bless us with Love's hues,
reminding us how to heal history's residues.
Masai Holy Ones ground Visions with their moves.

Samurai, Druids and Braveheart—claim your due.
Star Nations of all directions, make your way through.
The Dervishes and Tribes of all nations whirl blankets too,
Blankets of Light for the next waves coming to you.
All Grandmothers and Grandfathers come into view.
Angels and Archangels, we recognize you too.
Seers, Knowers, and Way Showers get thanks overdue.
Ancient Ones sing from mountains they once knew.

Stand up for love; love, Pure Love so true.
Stand up and love all as Creator Loves you.
Stand up for generations, past and future too.
Malcolm, Rosa, Martin and Fannie Lou—
those who give their lives for Love, Light
and freedom, we honor you—
Gandhi, Howard Thurman, Mother Theresa,
Dalai Lamas and Tiananmen Warriors too.
Wounded Knee, Dog Soldiers, Light Protectors come anew.
Harriett Tubman and Underground Conductors,
for your Vision, Love and Courage, we salute you.

Wounds come from lessons, and lessons come from wounds.
Wrap ourselves in blankets, as our lives are renewed.
Stand up. Stand up. Stand up.
I—send—my—blankets—over—you. ♥

Reflections:

Reflections:

Chapter Seven.

Epilogue

And so we search for Union and we search through Love.
Separation is the lie before we see the Wholeness—
from within, below and above:

I am the King's Daughter,
the Daughter of the Chief.
I show Ways of Knowing and Doing,
seeds and fruits of our beliefs.

Look 'round at what we've grown,
with all others and quite alone,
shapes of substance from our vast deep ground.

See our choices and our deeds,
wishes shaped by fiery dreams,
visions of our minds' inner eyes.

Search spaces where we care,
digging for roots buried there,
beneath the worn patterns we have grown.

Face what each of us most fears,
a cure within is coming near,
the Unknown becomes the Known again.

Beneath our urgent cries
lurked an illusion and a lie
hiding Truths each of us can own.

Dance upon the sunset's ground,
to holy drumming healing sounds,
layers of illusions now drop and dissolve.

Now, all debts we can atone and resolve:

What is the wound you now want to be healed?
What is the lie you'll no longer conceal?
What is the urgent dream you want to make real?
What is the part of you yearning most to be revealed?

How has it served you to keep all this sealed?
Is it time to surrender to the forces that heal?

What is the wound that is now being healed?
What is the Truth that no longer is concealed?
What is the urgent Dream that is now being made real?
What is the part of you now being revealed?

Unleash Pure Love stored beneath the Heart's Great Seal.
Circulate Pure Love within. Use all your zeal.

Having earned the right to say:

"I have healed the wound that wants to be healed.
I am speaking the Truths that are now revealed.
I am living the Dreams my soul wants to make real.
I am expressing my True Self, wanting to be revealed.
It is time to serve the people with all my zeal."

Who am I?

I am the King's Daughter,
the Daughter of the Chief.
I show Ways of Knowing and Doing,
seeds and fruits of our beliefs. ༄

Some of the Lessons of Love

"Love Economics running through all domains, a current of life force joining all planes."

"I am the Prize and We are the Prize when We Love Purely and Do as God devises."

"Power is the medicine we're all makin' with the medicine we're all takin'.."

"Blankets of Light are Love's vibration and Truth is Love's conversation."

"Everybody's lookin' for that Mother-Father kind o' love. Aren't you?"

"Love the Heart of a Tyrant, the obsessed, controlling woman or man."

"I trust you to be who you are. I trust me to see who you are."

"Love's greatest tests come before Love's greatest testimonies."

"….I learned to swim in the mercy of my own heart's sea."

"Child of Love's Hope, parent the self. Be born again."

"There is Love for the Unloved Lover in You and Me."

"Love can feed the many, making little into plenty."

"Pure Love is its own total and complete exchange."

"Pure Love marries Genius and Feminine Fire."

"Love is the Power, moving everything."

"Eat a ripe peach from your own tree."

"Be Love, Beloved".

The Reflect Upon The Rock Collection
Darya Funches, Ed.D.

A Collection of Poems, Stories and Songs for Healing,
Transformation and Co-Creating New Realities

Volume One.

I Send My Blankets Over You
Lessons of Love

Volume Two.

From the Disinherited to the Chosen
Lessons of Privilege & Oppression

Volume Three.

Leadership is an Initiation
Lessons in Visionary Leadership

Volume Four.

Songs for a Prayer Feather
Lessons on Spirit in the Material World

Look for Volumes Two, Three and Four in 2006 and 2007
and Companion Books for each of the Volumes
with Concepts, Examples and Exercises.

And

<u>Three Gifts—Awaken the Leader Within</u>
<u>Discernment, Heart and Presence</u>

About the Author

Darya Funches, Ed.D. is a consultant, coach, speaker and teacher of Visionary Leadership, Spirit in the Workplace, Personal and Corporate Transformation, Large Systems Change and the Science of Creating Reality. She is a skilled practitioner who designs and conducts corporate, spiritual and personal experiences to help clients heal their pasts and unfold their futures. Often referred to as a "consultant's consultant," Darya is a resource for accurate diagnosis and assessment, strategic direction and choices for achieving specific results.

After a seven year spiritual sabbatical and a 30 year career in leadership, corporate and personal transformation, this is the first in a series of books. She launches the <u>Reflect upon the Rock Collection</u> with <u>I Send My Blankets</u> <u>Over You—Lessons of Love</u>. At a time where change and transformation are critical to all of us, Darya brings her work from behind the scenes to make it available to the people.

She is currently interested in co-creating new forms of business for the 21st century, applying the approaches she has developed to specific social change and justice issues, and developing visionary leaders across different sectors and disciplines. Darya weaves the scientific, spiritual, psychological and the arts together in her work. She is a member and faculty of the Gestalt Institute of Cleveland, Adjunct Faculty for the Union Institute for Graduate Studies, a member of the National Organization Development Network and the International Hypnosis Federation. As former Chairperson of the Board of NTL Institute for Applied Behavioral Science and former Adjunct Faculty at American University and University of Southern California-WPAC, she has been an educator for many leaders and change agents.

Darya lives in Washington State and travels in the US and abroad assisting others. She also works with clients from her Retreat Center, Mossyrock Landing, in Washington, which she affectionately calls "The Rock." This Collection was written mostly from this place. Her hobbies are writing, cooking, walking, music, dancing, traveling and films.

Other Works and Publications

Funches, D., "Three Gifts of the Organization Development Practitioner," in Sykes and Drexler, eds. Emerging Theory and Practice of Organization Development. University Associates and NTL Institute, Publishers.

Marshall, L. and Funches, D., "Leadership is Love Made Visible," A Conversation with Darya Funches, in Marshall, L., Speak the Truth and Point to Hope. Kendall-Hunt Publishers.

Funches, D. The Inner Experience of Transformation: A Study in Use of Self as an Instrument of Transformation. Unpublished Dissertation. University of Massachusetts School of Education.